WILLIAMS-SONOMA

PIE & TART

RECIPES AND TEXT
CAROLYN BETH WEIL

GENERAL EDITOR
CHUCK WILLIAMS

PHOTOGRAPHS
MAREN CARUSO

SIMON & SCHUSTER • **SOURCE**

NEW YORK • LONDON • TORONTO • SYDNEY • SINGAPORE

CONTENTS

SIMPLE PIES

ELEGANT TARTS

RUSTIC TARTS

INTRODUCTION

Simple and delicious, a freshly baked pie or tart represents home cooking at its best. Yet, despite their homey appearances, there are a few tricks to making pies or tarts from scratch. For this reason, I urge you to turn to the basics section at the back of this book before you begin making the recipes inside. Here, you will find all you need to know about the right equipment and ingredients to use, as well as detailed explanations of techniques that will yield the best results. Armed with this information and a little practice, you will soon uncover the secrets to crisp, flaky crusts and sweet, juicy fillings.

In addition, each of the kitchen-tested recipes inside highlights a particular ingredient, term, or technique to help you deepen your knowledge of baking. So whether you prefer a slice from an old-fashioned apple pie, a beautiful chocolate tart, or a rustic galette made with fresh figs, these recipes are sure to become trusted favorites in your kitchen for many years to come.

THE CLASSICS

Whether based on fresh fruit, rich nuts, or irresistible chocolate and ice cream, the delicious and unique combinations of ingredients that these classic recipes contain have earned them a permanent place among our most well-loved desserts. The recipes that follow represent the many different styles of making pies and tarts, and each, in its own way, recalls one of our time-honored favorites.

APPLE PIE

CRIMPING

"Crimping" means sealing together the edges of a double-crust pie to prevent the filling from oozing out as it bubbles up in the heat of the oven. First, fold the overhang of the top crust under the overhang of the bottom crust, then press them together with the tines of a fork, the flat side of a knife blade, a specialized tool called a pastry crimper, or your fingers. Dip the tool or your fingers in flour to prevent sticking if necessary, and be careful not to poke holes in the top crust. An edge may also be crimped and then fluted, shaped with your fingers into a scallop or similar pattern (page 107).

Fold 1 dough round in half and carefully transfer to a 9-inch (23-cm) pie pan or dish. Unfold and ease the round into the pan, without stretching it, and pat it firmly into the bottom and up the sides of the pan. Using kitchen scissors, trim the edge of the dough, leaving ¾ inch (2 cm) of overhang. Set the dough-lined pan aside, along with the second dough round, in a cool place until ready to use.

In a small bowl, stir together the sugar, cinnamon, salt, and flour. Place the sliced apples in a large bowl, sprinkle with the sugar mixture, and toss to distribute evenly. Pile the apples into the dough-lined pan. Dot them with the butter.

Fold the reserved dough round in half and carefully position over half of the filled pie. Unfold and trim the edge neatly, leaving 1 inch (2.5 cm) of overhang, then fold the edge of the top round under the edge of the bottom round and crimp the edges to seal *(left)*. Using a small, sharp knife, cut 5 or 6 slits in the top to allow steam to escape during baking.

Refrigerate the pie until the dough is firm, 20–30 minutes. Meanwhile, place an oven rack in the lower third of the oven and preheat to 350°F (180°C).

Bake the pie until the crust is golden and the apples are tender when pierced through a vent with a skewer or long, thin knife, 60–70 minutes. Transfer the pie to a wire rack and let cool until just slightly warm, about 45 minutes, before serving. If desired, accompany each serving with a scoop of vanilla ice cream.

MAKES ONE 9-INCH (23-CM) PIE, OR 8 SERVINGS

2 rolled-out Basic Pie Dough rounds (page 110)

½ cup (4 oz/125 g) sugar

½ teaspoon ground cinnamon

⅛ teaspoon salt

1 tablespoon unbleached all-purpose (plain) flour

7 large, tart, firm apples (page 40), peeled, halved lengthwise, cored, and sliced ½ inch (12 mm) thick (about 6 cups)

2 tablespoons cold unsalted butter, cut into small pieces

Vanilla ice cream for serving (optional)

CHERRY PIE

1 rolled-out Basic Pie Dough round and 1 rolled-out Basic Pie Dough rectangle (page 110)

1 cup (8 oz/250 g) sugar

3 tablespoons cornstarch (cornflour)

¼ teaspoon salt

4 cups (24 oz/750 g) drained jarred or canned pitted sour cherries plus ⅓ cup (3 fl oz/80 ml) cherry liquid

1 teaspoon vanilla extract (essence)

2 tablespoons cold unsalted butter, cut into small pieces

Fold 1 dough round in half and carefully transfer to a 9-inch (23-cm) pie pan or dish. Unfold and ease the round into the pan, without stretching it, and pat it firmly into the bottom and up the sides of the pan. Using kitchen scissors, trim the edge of the dough, leaving ¾ inch (2 cm) of overhang. Set the dough-lined pan aside, along with the dough rectangle, in a cool place until ready to use.

In a small bowl, stir together the sugar, cornstarch, and salt. Place the cherries in a large bowl, sprinkle with the sugar mixture, and toss to distribute evenly. Add the vanilla and the cherry liquid and mix well. Immediately transfer the cherry mixture to the dough-lined pan and dot with the butter.

Use the dough rectangle to make a lattice top as directed on page 109.

Refrigerate the pie until the dough is firm, 20–30 minutes. Meanwhile, place an oven rack in the middle of the oven and preheat to 425°F (220°C).

Bake the pie for 15 minutes. Reduce the oven temperature to 350°F (180°C) and continue to bake until the crust is golden and the filling is thick and bubbling, 40–50 minutes longer. Transfer the pie to a wire rack and let cool completely. Serve the pie at room temperature.

Serving Tips: To serve the pie warm, reheat in a 350°F (180°C) oven for 10–12 minutes. If desired, accompany each serving with a scoop of vanilla or toasted almond ice cream.

MAKES ONE 9-INCH (23-CM) PIE. OR 8 SERVINGS

CHERRIES

Cherries come in two primary types: sweet and sour (or tart). Sour cherries need to be cooked before eating and are most readily found processed and jarred for use in pie filling, or made into preserves or juice. You can also make this pie with pitted fresh sweet cherries. Replace the jarred sour cherries with 4 cups (24 oz/750 g) fresh sweet cherries, reduce the sugar to ¾ cup (6 oz/185 g), and add ½ teaspoon almond extract (essence). During their short summer season, look for large, plump, smooth cherries that are darkly colored for their variety and preferably still have their stems attached.

13

FRUIT TART WITH PASTRY CREAM

Fold the dough round in half and transfer to a 9½-inch (24-cm) tart pan, preferably with a removable bottom. Unfold and ease into the pan, patting it firmly into the bottom and up the sides. Trim off any excess dough. Press the dough into the sides to extend it slightly above the rim. Refrigerate or freeze the tart shell until firm, about 30 minutes. Place an oven rack in the lower third of the oven and preheat to 375°F (190°C). Fully bake the tart shell as directed on page 109. Transfer to a wire rack and let cool.

To make the pastry cream, in a nonaluminum saucepan over medium heat, warm the milk until tiny bubbles appear on the surface, 6–8 minutes. In a bowl, whisk together the egg yolks and sugar. Add the cornstarch and salt. Pour in half of the hot milk while whisking constantly. Whisk in the remaining milk and return to the saucepan. Cook over medium heat, whisking constantly, until the mixture thickens to a firm consistency, 5–8 minutes. Scrape into a bowl. Whisk in the vanilla. Cover with plastic wrap, pressing it directly onto the surface of the pastry cream. Refrigerate for 2–3 hours.

To assemble the tart, stir the pastry cream with a rubber spatula until smooth. Spoon into the bottom of the baked tart shell and spread evenly. Overlap the mango slices in a ring around the rim of the tart. Arrange the strawberry halves, cut sides down, in a second ring and the raspberries in a third ring. Overlap the kiwifruit slices in a fourth ring. Fill the center with the blueberries.

In a saucepan over low heat, heat the jam until it liquefies. Pour through a fine-mesh sieve set over a small bowl. Using a pastry brush, gently brush the fruit with a thin coating of the jam. If using a tart pan with a removable bottom, let the sides fall away (page 105), then slide the tart onto a serving plate. Refrigerate until ready to serve, then let sit at room temperature for 20 minutes.

MAKES ONE 9½-INCH (24-CM) TART, OR 8 SERVINGS

TEMPERING EGGS

To prevent beaten eggs from curdling when they are added to hot liquid, they must first be tempered, or heated slightly. This is an important step when making pastry cream, custard, or any sauce that calls for uncooked eggs and a hot liquid such as cream or milk. To temper eggs, beat them lightly until blended, then whisk in a little of the hot liquid to raise their temperature. Gradually add the remaining hot cream while whisking constantly. At this point, the liquid can then be returned to the stove for further heating.

1 rolled-out Basic Tart Dough round (page 111)

FOR THE PASTRY CREAM:

2 cups (16 fl oz/500 ml) whole milk

6 large egg yolks

½ cup (4 oz/125 g) sugar

¼ cup (1 oz/30 g) cornstarch (cornflour)

⅛ teaspoon salt

1 teaspoon vanilla extract (essence)

FOR THE TOPPING:

1 mango, peeled, pitted, and cut into slices ¼ inch (6 mm) thick

2 cups (8 oz/250 g) strawberries, hulled and halved lengthwise

2 cups (8 oz/250 g) raspberries

2 or 3 kiwifruits, peeled, halved lengthwise, and cut crosswise into slices ¼ inch (6 mm) thick

½ cup (2 oz/60 g) blueberries

⅓ cup (3½ oz/105 g) apricot jam

KEY LIME PIE

FOR THE FILLING:

7 large egg yolks

4 teaspoons finely grated Key lime zest

2 cans (14 fl oz/430 ml each) sweetened condensed milk

1 cup (8 fl oz/250 ml) fresh Key lime juice, strained (about 24 limes)

1 Cookie Crumb Crust (page 110), made with graham crackers

Sweetened Whipped Cream (page 111)

Place an oven rack in the lower third of the oven and preheat to 350°F (180°C).

To make the filling, in a bowl, whisk together the egg yolks and lime zest until well mixed, about 1 minute. Add the condensed milk and then the lime juice, whisking well after each addition. Pour the filling into the graham cracker crust.

Bake until the filling is firm in the center, 20–24 minutes. Transfer to a wire rack and let cool completely. Refrigerate until cold and firm, 2–3 hours.

Using a pastry bag (page 111), pipe 8 large rosettes or a zigzag of whipped cream evenly around the edge of the pie. Refrigerate until ready to serve, but let sit at room temperature for 20 minutes before serving, to take the chill off.

Variation Tip: Try adding 2 tablespoons tequila to the filling along with the lime juice.

MAKES ONE 9-INCH (23-CM) PIE, OR 8 SERVINGS

KEY LIMES

Key limes, also known as Mexican and West Indian limes, are small, round, and pale green to yellow, with mild juice, thin skin, and an abundance of seeds. Some of these walnut-sized citrus are grown in the Florida Keys, Texas, and California, but they are more widely produced in Mexico and Central America. Good-quality bottled Key lime juice is also available. If you cannot find fresh Key limes or bottled Key lime juice, you can make this pie with more common Persian limes. You will need about 10 limes for 1 cup juice. Persian limes will produce a more tart pie, however.

LEMON MERINGUE PIE

MERINGUE

In a saucepan, whisk together 1 tablespoon cornstarch (cornflour) and ¼ cup (2 fl oz/60 ml) water. Cook over medium heat, stirring constantly, until thick, about 2 minutes. Let cool. In a bowl, using an electric mixer on high speed, whip 4 large egg whites and ½ teaspoon cream of tartar until foamy. Reduce the speed to medium and whip while sprinkling in ½ cup (4 oz/125 g) sugar. Return to high speed and whip until the whites form a ribbon that folds back on itself when the beater is raised. Stir in the cornstarch mixture and beat on high speed until shiny and soft peaks form, 2–3 minutes.

If using pie dough, fold the dough round in half and transfer to a 9-inch (23-cm) pie pan or dish. Unfold and ease into the pan, patting it firmly into the bottom and up the sides. Trim the edge of the dough, leaving ¾ inch (2 cm) of overhang. Fold the overhang under itself and pinch to create a high edge on the pan's rim; flute decoratively (page 107). Refrigerate or freeze the pie shell until firm, about 30 minutes. Place an oven rack in the lower third of the oven and preheat to 375°F (190°C). Fully bake the pie shell as directed on page 109. Transfer to a wire rack and let cool. Move the oven rack to the middle of the oven.

To make the filling, in a bowl, whisk together the whole eggs, egg yolks, and sugar until pale yellow. Add the cornstarch and salt. Stir in the lemon juice, water, butter, and lemon zest. Transfer to a saucepan and cook over medium heat, stirring constantly, until very thick and erupting with large bubbles, 7–9 minutes. Remove from the heat and stir for 1 minute to make sure the filling is completely thickened. Spread the filling evenly in the crust, and press a piece of plastic wrap directly onto the surface. Refrigerate for 2–3 hours.

Heap the meringue onto the filling and, using a rubber spatula or spoon, spread it to the edges and seal it to the crust. With the back of a small spoon, gently lift the surface of the meringue to create small peaks. Bake the pie until the meringue is a light golden brown, 15–18 minutes. Transfer to a wire rack and let stand until the meringue is cool, at least 30 minutes, before serving.

Notes: Meringues attract moisture and will eventually sweat and shrink, so serve this pie the day it is made. Note that this meringue contains semicooked egg whites; for more information, see page 113.

MAKES ONE 9-INCH (23-CM) PIE, OR 8 SERVINGS

1 rolled-out Basic Pie Dough round (page 110) or 1 Cookie Crumb Crust (page 110), made with graham crackers

FOR THE FILLING:

2 large whole eggs, plus 4 large egg yolks

1½ cups (12 oz/375 g) sugar

¼ cup (1 oz/30 g) cornstarch (cornflour)

Pinch of salt

1 cup (8 fl oz/250 ml) fresh lemon juice, strained (from about 7 large lemons)

¼ cup (2 fl oz/60 ml) water

3 tablespoons unsalted butter, cut into small pieces

1 tablespoon finely grated lemon zest

Meringue *(far left)*

MAPLE-PECAN PIE

1 rolled-out Basic Pie Dough round (page 110)

2 cups (22 oz/690 g) maple syrup

2 large eggs, lightly beaten

¼ cup (2 oz/60 g) firmly packed light or dark brown sugar

⅛ teaspoon salt

2 tablespoons unsalted butter, melted

1 teaspoon vanilla extract (essence)

1½ cups (6 oz/185 g) pecans, coarsely chopped

Fold the dough round in half and carefully transfer to a 9-inch (23-cm) pie pan or dish. Unfold and ease the round into the pan, without stretching it, and pat it into the bottom and firmly up the sides of the pan. Using kitchen scissors, trim the edge of the dough, leaving ¾ inch (2 cm) of overhang. Fold the overhang under itself and pinch it together to create a high edge on the pan's rim. Flute the edge decoratively (page 107).

Refrigerate or freeze the pie shell until firm, about 30 minutes. Meanwhile, place an oven rack in the lower third of the oven and preheat to 375°F (190°C).

Partially bake the pie shell as directed on page 109. Transfer to a wire rack. Reduce the oven temperature to 350°F (180°C).

In a saucepan over medium-high heat, bring the maple syrup to a boil and boil for 8–10 minutes to reduce. Remove from the heat and pour into a heatproof measuring pitcher. The syrup should be reduced to 1½ cups (12 oz/375 g). If necessary, return the syrup to the saucepan and continue to boil until sufficiently reduced. Let cool to room temperature before proceeding.

In a bowl, stir together the eggs, brown sugar, reduced maple syrup, salt, melted butter, and vanilla until well mixed. Add the pecans and stir well. Pour into the partially baked pie shell, making sure the pecans are evenly distributed.

Bake the pie until the center is slightly puffed and firm to the touch, 30–35 minutes. Transfer to a wire rack and let cool until just slightly warm, about 45 minutes, before serving.

Serving Tips: Serve with Sweetened Whipped Cream (page 111). Flavor the cream with 1 tablespoon bourbon, if desired.

MAKES ONE 9-INCH (23-CM) PIE, OR 8 SERVINGS

MAPLE SYRUP

Pure maple syrup, made from the boiled sap of the sugar maple tree, comes in three grades. Grade A Light or Fancy syrup, sometimes called Grade AA, is clear gold and has a wonderfully subtle flavor, but its delicate character does not hold up in cooking. Grade B syrup is produced only in Vermont and has more maple flavor than Grade A. Sometimes called "baking" or "cooking" maple syrup, it is ideal for use in this recipe. Grade C has a robust, molasses-like flavor and is used primarily in making commercial table syrups.

BANANA CREAM PIE

Fold the dough round in half and transfer to a 9-inch (23-cm) pie pan or dish. Unfold and ease into the pan, patting it firmly into the bottom and up the sides. Trim the edge of the dough, leaving ¾ inch (2 cm) of overhang. Fold the overhang under itself and pinch to create a high edge on the pan's rim; flute decoratively (page 107). Refrigerate or freeze the pie shell until firm, about 30 minutes. Place an oven rack in the lower third of the oven and preheat to 375°F (190°C). Fully bake the pie shell as directed on page 109. Transfer to a wire rack and let cool completely.

To make the filling, pour the cold water into a small bowl and sprinkle with the gelatin. Let sit until the gelatin softens and swells, 5–10 minutes. In a saucepan over medium heat, warm the milk until hot to the touch, about 8 minutes. Remove from the heat. In a bowl, whisk together the egg yolks and sugar until pale yellow. Add the cornstarch and salt, beating until smooth. Add the hot milk to the yolk mixture 1 cup (8 fl oz/250 ml) at a time, mixing well after each addition. Add the softened gelatin and mix well. Return to the saucepan over medium heat and cook, stirring constantly, until the mixture thickens and begins to bubble, 8–9 minutes. Remove from the heat and whisk in the vanilla.

Lay two-thirds of the banana slices in a single layer in the bottom of the baked pie shell. Stir the remaining slices into the custard and spoon it evenly over the bananas. Cover with plastic wrap. Prick a few holes in the plastic. Refrigerate for about 4 hours.

To make the topping, in a large bowl, combine the cream, rum (if using), vanilla, and sugar. Using an electric mixer on medium-high speed, beat until soft peaks form. Spread the whipped cream on top of the cooled pie. Refrigerate until ready to serve, then let sit at room temperature for 20 minutes.

MAKES ONE 9-INCH (23-CM) PIE, OR 8 SERVINGS

1 rolled-out Basic Pie Dough round (page 110)

FOR THE FILLING:

¼ cup (2 fl oz/60 ml) cold water

2¼ teaspoons (1 package) unflavored powdered gelatin

2 cups (16 fl oz/500 ml) whole milk

4 large egg yolks

½ cup (4 oz/125 g) sugar

¼ cup (1 oz/30 g) cornstarch (cornflour)

¼ teaspoon salt

1 teaspoon vanilla extract (essence)

3 bananas, peeled and cut into slices ½ inch (12 mm) thick

FOR THE TOPPING:

1 cup (8 fl oz/250 ml) heavy (double) cream

1 tablespoon dark rum (optional)

1 teaspoon vanilla extract (essence)

1 tablespoon sugar

MISSISSIPPI MUD PIE

1 cup (6 oz/185 g) semi-sweet (plain) chocolate chips

4 tablespoons (2 oz/60 g) unsalted butter

¼ cup (2 fl oz/60 ml) heavy (double) cream

2 tablespoons light corn syrup

1 cup (4 oz/125 g) confectioners' (icing) sugar, sifted

1 teaspoon vanilla extract (essence)

1 Cookie Crumb Crust (page 110), made with chocolate cookies

½ cup (2½ oz/75 g) toffee bits or coarsely chopped toasted almonds (page 114, see Note)

1 qt (1 l) premium coffee ice cream, softened

In the top of a double boiler *(right)*, combine the chocolate chips, butter, cream, and corn syrup. Set over, but not touching, barely simmering water in the bottom pan until the chocolate is melted, stirring occasionally. Alternatively, in a microwaveproof bowl, combine the chocolate, butter, cream, and corn syrup and melt in the microwave for 30-second intervals. Remove from the microwave and stir until smooth.

Add the confectioners' sugar and vanilla to the chocolate mixture and mix well. Reserve ½ cup (4 fl oz/125 ml) of the chocolate mixture for the top of the pie. Spread the remaining mixture evenly in the bottom of the cookie crust. Sprinkle with half of the toffee bits. Refrigerate until well chilled, about 1 hour.

In a large bowl, using an electric mixer on medium speed, beat the ice cream until it is spreadable but not runny. Immediately mound into the pie shell and spread evenly. Freeze until the ice cream is firm, at least 2 hours or for up to overnight.

Reheat the reserved chocolate mixture in the top of the double boiler over barely simmering water, or in the microwave for 30-second intervals, until it is spreadable but not hot. Using a spatula, spread it over the ice cream. Sprinkle with the remaining toffee bits and return the pie to the freezer until it is completely firm before serving, 3–4 hours. To slice, run a knife under hot water, then dry it off. If frozen overnight, the pie may need to sit out for a few minutes before it is soft enough to slice easily.

Note: You can find packaged toffee bits in the baking section of well-stocked markets, or chop up a toffee candy bar. The toffee bits make this pie a special treat, especially for children. For a more sophisticated version, use toasted almonds.

MAKES ONE 9-INCH (23-CM) PIE, OR 8 SERVINGS

DOUBLE BOILER

A double boiler is used for cooking foods gently on the stove top. Made up of two nesting saucepans, double boilers are available in cook-ware stores, but a makeshift one is easy to assemble. Choose a saucepan and a heatproof bowl that rests securely in the top of the pan. Fill the saucepan with water to a depth of 1–2 inches (2.5–5 cm). Once the bowl is placed atop the pan, the water must not touch the bowl; allow at least 2 inches (5 cm) of clearance. Bring the water to a boil, set the bowl in place, and reduce the heat so that the water simmers gently.

FRUIT PIES

Bakers eagerly await the arrival of warm weather for the abundance of fresh, sweet fruits that comes with it. There is simply no substitute for the plump, deep-hued berries and fragrant stone fruits of summer, or for the crisp and tart apples that arrive as autumn approaches. At their peak of ripeness, these delicious fruits can be used to fill pies we look forward to enjoying year after year.

SUMMER BERRY PIE
28

BLUEBERRY PIE
31

GEORGIA PEACH PIE
32

STRAWBERRY-RHUBARB PIE
35

GINGER-APRICOT PIE
36

DEEP-DISH PLUM PIE
39

APPLE PANDOWDY PIE
40

SUMMER BERRY PIE

HANDLING BERRIES

HANDLING BERRIES

While some berries can be found in the market year-round, most will taste best in the summer, their natural season. Select plump berries with deep color and bright flavor. Just before using, sort through them carefully and remove and discard any that are blemished or moldy. Gently rinse the berries under cold running water, but do not allow them to soak for any length of time, as they quickly absorb moisture and will turn mushy. Lay the rinsed berries in a single layer on paper towels to dry.

Fold 1 dough round in half and carefully transfer to a 9-inch (23-cm) pie pan or dish. Unfold and ease the round into the pan, without stretching it, and pat it firmly into the bottom and up the sides of the pan. Using kitchen scissors, trim the edge of the dough, leaving ¾ inch (2 cm) of overhang. Set the dough-lined pan aside, along with the second dough round, in a cool place until ready to use.

In a small bowl, stir together the sugar, cornstarch, tapioca, cinnamon, and salt. Place the berries in a large bowl, sprinkle with the sugar mixture, and toss to distribute evenly. Immediately transfer to the dough-lined pan. Dot with the butter.

Fold the reserved dough round in half and carefully position over half of the filled pie. Unfold and trim the edge neatly, leaving 1 inch (2.5 cm) of overhang, then fold the edge of the top round under the edge of the bottom round and crimp the edges to seal (page 10). Using a small, round cookie cutter or a small, sharp knife, cut 5 or 6 holes or slits in the top crust to allow steam to escape during baking.

Refrigerate the pie until the dough is firm, 20–30 minutes. Meanwhile, place an oven rack in the lower third of the oven and preheat to 350°F (180°C).

Bake the pie until the crust is golden and the filling is thick and bubbling, 50–60 minutes. Transfer to a wire rack and let cool completely to set. Serve at room temperature or rewarm in a 350°F (180°C) oven for 10–15 minutes just before serving.

MAKES ONE 9-INCH (23-CM) PIE, OR 8 SERVINGS

2 rolled-out Basic Pie Dough rounds (page 110)

1 cup (8 oz/250 g) sugar

2 tablespoons cornstarch (cornflour)

2 tablespoons quick-cooking tapioca

½ teaspoon ground cinnamon

Pinch of salt

6 cups (1½ lb/750 g) mixed fresh berries, such as blackberries, blueberries, raspberries, and/or boysenberries

1 tablespoon cold unsalted butter, cut into small pieces

BLUEBERRY PIE

2 rolled-out Basic Pie
Dough rounds (page 110)

4 cups (1 lb/500 g)
blueberries

1 tablespoon fresh lemon
juice, strained

¾ cup (6 oz/185 g) sugar

3 tablespoons cornstarch
(cornflour)

½ teaspoon finely grated
lemon zest

¼ teaspoon salt

¼ teaspoon ground
cinnamon

1 tablespoon cold unsalted
butter, cut into small
pieces

Fold 1 dough round in half and carefully transfer to a 9-inch (23-cm) pie pan or dish. Unfold and ease the round into the pan, without stretching it, and pat it firmly into the bottom and up the sides of the pan. Using kitchen scissors, trim the edge of the dough, leaving ¾ inch (2 cm) of overhang. Set the dough-lined pan aside, along with the second dough round, in a cool place until ready to use.

Place the berries in a large bowl, sprinkle with the lemon juice, and toss to coat evenly. In a small bowl, stir together the sugar, cornstarch, lemon zest, salt, and cinnamon. Sprinkle the sugar mixture over the berries and toss to distribute evenly. Immediately transfer to the dough-lined pan. Dot with the butter.

Fold the reserved dough round in half and carefully position over half of the filled pie. Unfold and trim the edge neatly, leaving 1 inch (2.5 cm) of overhang, then fold the edge of the top round under the edge of the bottom round and crimp the edges to seal (page 10). Using a small, sharp knife, cut an asterisk 4–5 inches (10–13 cm) across in the center of the top to allow steam to escape during baking.

Refrigerate the pie until the dough is firm, 20–30 minutes. Meanwhile, place an oven rack in the lower third of the oven and preheat to 375°F (190°C).

Bake the pie until the crust is golden and the filling is thick and bubbling, 50–60 minutes. Transfer to a wire rack and let cool completely to set, 1–2 hours. Serve at room temperature or rewarm in a 350°F (180°C) oven for 10–15 minutes just before serving.

Note: If fresh blueberries are unavailable, use frozen blueberries (without thawing them first) and increase the baking time by 10–15 minutes.

MAKES ONE 9-INCH (23-CM) PIE, OR 8 SERVINGS

ZESTING AND JUICING

When a recipe calls for citrus zest and juice, always begin by zesting the rind. First, scrub the fruit well to remove any wax or chemicals. If possible, buy organic fruit to use for zesting. Use a zester, vegetable peeler, or fine Microplane grater to remove just the thin, colored portion of the rind, being careful not to include the bitter white pith underneath. To juice, slice the fruit in half crosswise. Working over a bowl, use a reamer to extract the juice or use a citrus juicer. Strain the juice before using to remove any seeds and pulp.

GEORGIA PEACH PIE

PEELING PEACHES

Whether or not to peel peaches for a pie is up to the baker. Some cooks feel the skins add color and flavor to the finished pie; others prefer the smooth texture of peeled peaches. A quick way to peel peaches or other thin-skinned fruits is to blanch them. Score the bottom (blossom end) of each peach with an X. In small batches, immerse the peaches in boiling water until the skins begin to curl at the X, 20–60 seconds. Immediately transfer to a bowl of ice water to cool. Using your fingertips, slip off the skins. Use a paring knife to remove any skin that resists coming away easily.

Fold 1 dough round in half and carefully transfer to a 9-inch (23-cm) pie pan or dish. Unfold and ease the round into the pan, without stretching it, and pat it firmly into the bottom and up the sides of the pan. Using kitchen scissors, trim the edge of the dough, leaving ¾ inch (2 cm) of overhang. Set the dough-lined pan aside, along with the second dough round, in a cool place until ready to use.

In a small bowl, stir together the sugar, cornstarch, tapioca, cinnamon, and salt. Place the peaches in a large bowl, sprinkle with the sugar mixture, and toss to distribute evenly. Immediately transfer to the dough-lined pan. Dot with the butter.

Fold the reserved dough round in half and carefully position over half of the filled pie. Unfold and trim the edge neatly, leaving 1 inch (2.5 cm) of overhang, then fold the edge of the top round under the edge of the bottom round and crimp the edges with your fingers to seal (page 10). Using a small, sharp knife, make slices around the edge of the crust, leaving about 1 inch (2.5 cm) between each slice. Fold every other slice up toward the center of the pie to create a decorative edge. Use the knife to cut 5 or 6 slits in the top crust to allow steam to escape.

Refrigerate the pie until the dough is firm, 20–30 minutes. Meanwhile, place an oven rack in the lower third of the oven and preheat to 375°F (190°C).

Bake the pie until the crust is golden and the filling is thick and bubbling, 50–60 minutes. Transfer to a wire rack and let cool completely to set. Serve at room temperature or rewarm in a 350°F (180°C) oven for 10–15 minutes just before serving.

Serving Tip: Serve with a drizzle of heavy (double) cream or a dollop of crème fraîche.

MAKES ONE 9-INCH (23-CM) PIE, OR 8 SERVINGS

2 rolled-out Basic Pie Dough rounds (page 110)

¾ cup (6 oz/185 g) sugar

2 tablespoons cornstarch (cornflour)

2 tablespoons quick-cooking tapioca

1 teaspoon ground cinnamon

Pinch of salt

6 or 7 ripe but firm peaches, peeled *(far left)*, pitted, and sliced ½ inch (12 mm) thick (about 5 cups)

1 tablespoon cold unsalted butter, cut into small pieces

STRAWBERRY-RHUBARB PIE

2 rolled-out Basic Pie Dough rounds (page 110)

1 cup (8 oz/250 g) sugar

2 tablespoons cornstarch (cornflour)

2 tablespoons quick-cooking tapioca

Pinch of salt

3 cups (12 oz/375 g) strawberries, hulled and quartered lengthwise

3 cups rhubarb (12 oz/375 g), trimmed and sliced ½ inch (12 mm) thick (about 4 or 5 stalks)

1 tablespoon cold unsalted butter, cut into small pieces

Fold 1 dough round in half and carefully transfer to a 9-inch (23-cm) pie pan or dish. Unfold and ease the round into the pan, without stretching it, and pat it firmly into the bottom and up the sides of the pan. Using kitchen scissors, trim the edge of the dough, leaving ¾ inch (2 cm) of overhang and reserving any dough scraps. Set the dough-lined pan aside, along with the second dough round, in a cool place until ready to use.

In a small bowl, stir together the sugar, cornstarch, tapioca, and salt. Place the strawberries and rhubarb in a large bowl, sprinkle with the sugar mixture, and toss to distribute evenly. Immediately transfer to the dough-lined pan. Dot with the butter.

Fold the reserved dough round in half and carefully position over half of the filled pie. Unfold and trim the edge neatly, leaving 1 inch (2.5 cm) of overhang, then fold the edge of the top round under the edge of the bottom round and crimp the edges to seal (page 10). Gather all of the dough scraps and roll out about ⅛ inch (3 mm) thick. Using a very small cookie cutter, cut out scalloped circles or other shapes of dough. Brush the edge of the crust and the undersides of the dough shapes with cold water and overlap the shapes around the edge of the pie. Using a small, sharp knife, cut 5 or 6 holes or slits in the top crust to allow steam to escape during baking.

Refrigerate the pie until the dough is firm, 20–30 minutes. Meanwhile, place an oven rack in the lower third of the oven and preheat to 350°F (180°C).

Bake the pie until the crust is golden and the filling is thick and bubbling, 50–60 minutes. Transfer to a wire rack and let cool completely to set. Serve at room temperature or rewarm in a 350°F (180°C) oven for 10–15 minutes just before serving.

MAKES ONE 9-INCH (23-CM) PIE, OR 8 SERVINGS

RHUBARB

Technically a vegetable, rhubarb is treated like a fruit and is traditionally paired with strawberries, which complement its tart, fruity flavor. Rhubarb comes in two types. Field rhubarb, most often available in late spring, is cherry-red and has a more pronounced flavor than its hothouse kin. Hothouse rhubarb is bright pink and is usually in the market year-round. To avoid a stringy filling, slice the rhubarb no wider than ½ inch (12 mm) thick. If the outside of the stalks are stringy, remove the strings with a vegetable peeler. Rhubarb leaves are mildly toxic and should always be discarded.

GINGER-APRICOT PIE

APRICOTS

Apricots, small cousins of the peach, are native to northern China, where they still grow wild today. They are cultivated in many warm climates worldwide, from California to the south of France, but have only a brief—and highly anticipated—season. Sweet and tangy, they are available from late spring to mid-summer. Look for apricots that are fragrant and have rich orange skin with a pink blush. If fully ripe, they give slightly when gently pressed. To hasten ripening, put the apricots in a paper bag along with a banana, then loosely close the bag.

Fold 1 dough round in half and carefully transfer to a 9-inch (23-cm) pie pan or dish. Unfold and ease the round into the pan, without stretching it, and pat it firmly into the bottom and up the sides of the pan. Using kitchen scissors, trim the edge of the dough, leaving ¾ inch (2 cm) of overhang. Set the dough-lined pan aside, along with the second dough round, in a cool place until ready to use.

In a small bowl, stir together the sugar, cornstarch, tapioca, ginger, cinnamon, and salt. Place the apricots in a large bowl, sprinkle with the orange zest and the sugar mixture, and toss to distribute evenly. Immediately transfer to the dough-lined pan. Dot with the butter.

Fold the reserved dough round in half and carefully position over half of the filled pie. Unfold and trim the edge neatly, leaving 1 inch (2.5 cm) of overhang, then fold the edge of the top round under the edge of the bottom round and crimp the edges to seal (page 10). Using a small, round cookie cutter or a small, sharp knife, cut 4 or 5 holes or slits in the top to allow steam to escape during baking.

Refrigerate the pie until the dough is firm, 20–30 minutes. Meanwhile, place an oven rack in the lower third of the oven and preheat to 375°F (190°C).

Bake the pie until the crust is golden and the filling is thick and bubbling, 50–60 minutes. Transfer to a wire rack and let cool completely to set. Serve at room temperature or rewarm in a 350°F (180°C) oven for 10–15 minutes just before serving.

MAKES ONE 9-INCH (23-CM) PIE, OR 8 SERVINGS

2 rolled-out Basic Pie Dough rounds (page 110)

¾ cup (6 oz/185 g) sugar

2 tablespoons cornstarch (cornflour)

2 tablespoons quick-cooking tapioca

1½ teaspoons ground ginger

1 teaspoon ground cinnamon

⅛ teaspoon salt

2 lb (1 kg) apricots, pitted and sliced ½ inch (12 mm) thick (about 5 cups)

1 teaspoon finely grated orange or lemon zest

1 tablespoon cold unsalted butter, cut into small pieces

DEEP-DISH PLUM PIE

1¼ cups (10 oz/315 g) sugar

3 tablespoons cornstarch (cornflour) or quick-cooking tapioca

½ teaspoon ground cinnamon

Pinch of salt

2½ lb (1.25 kg) plums, pitted and sliced ¼ inch (6 mm) thick (about 5 cups)

1 tablespoon cold unsalted butter, cut into small pieces

1 rolled-out Basic Pie Dough round (page 110)

Vanilla ice cream for serving (optional)

In a small bowl, stir together the sugar, cornstarch, cinnamon, and salt. Set aside. Place the plums in a large bowl, sprinkle with the sugar mixture, and toss to distribute evenly. Immediately transfer to a 10-inch (25-cm) ceramic or glass deep-dish pie dish. Dot with the butter.

Carefully position the dough round over the plums. Trim the edge neatly, leaving 1 inch (2.5 cm) of overhang, then place over the fruit, folding the overhang under and pressing against the sides of the dish to seal. Using a small, sharp knife, cut 5 or 6 slits in the top crust to allow steam to escape during baking.

Refrigerate the pie until the dough is firm, 20–30 minutes. Meanwhile, place an oven rack in the lower third of the oven and preheat to 375°F (190°C).

Bake the pie for 15 minutes. Reduce the oven temperature to 350°F (180°C) and continue to bake until the crust is golden and the filling is thick and bubbling, 50–60 minutes longer. Transfer to a wire rack and let cool completely. Serve at room temperature or rewarm in a 350°F (180°C) oven for 10–15 minutes just before serving. To serve, cut into wedges and spoon into individual serving bowls. If desired, accompany each serving with a scoop of vanilla ice cream.

MAKES ONE 10-INCH (25-CM) PIE, OR 8 SERVINGS

PLUM TYPES

Fresh plums are available from late spring through summer. You will find these juicy fruits in an assortment of colors, from yellow and green to deep pink, purple, and scarlet. Check out the varieties at your local farmers' market, and choose a firm, fragrant fruit with sweet, tangy flesh (such as Simka, Santa Rosa, Seneca, or Satsuma). The small, oval, purple-skinned, golden-fleshed plums known as Italian, French, or prune plums will also make a delicious pie.

APPLE PANDOWDY PIE

Fold 1 dough round in half and carefully transfer to a 9-inch (23-cm) pie pan or dish. Unfold and ease the round into the pan, without stretching it, and pat it firmly into the bottom and up the sides of the pan. Using kitchen scissors, trim the edge of the dough, leaving 1½–2 inches (4–5 cm) of overhang. Set the dough-lined pan aside, along with the second dough round, in a cool place until ready to use.

Place the sliced apples in a large bowl, sprinkle with the lemon juice, and toss to coat evenly. In a small bowl, stir together the brown sugar, cornstarch, cinnamon, nutmeg, and salt. Sprinkle the sugar mixture over the apples and toss to distribute. Pile into the dough-lined pan. Dot with the butter.

Trim the second dough round to a 9-inch (23-cm) circle. Fold in half and carefully position over half of the filled pie, then unfold the top round. Fold the bottom round up and over the top round, pleating the dough loosely all around the edge (page 97).

Refrigerate the pie until the dough is firm, 20–30 minutes. Meanwhile, place an oven rack in the lower third of the oven and preheat to 350°F (180°C).

Bake until the dough is set, about 30 minutes. Remove the pie from the oven and use a small, sharp knife to cut the top crust in a crisscross pattern, cutting it into rows of 1-inch (2.5 cm) squares. Using a flexible metal spatula, press the squares into the apples. Sprinkle with the granulated sugar. Continue baking the pie until the crust is golden and the apples are tender when pierced with a skewer or long, thin knife, 30–40 minutes longer. Transfer the pie to a wire rack and let cool for 30 minutes. To serve, cut into wedges and top with whipped cream or vanilla ice cream, if desired.

MAKES ONE 9-INCH (23-CM) PIE, OR 8 SERVINGS

2 rolled-out Basic Pie Dough rounds (page 110)

6 large, tart, firm apples *(far left),* peeled, halved lengthwise, cored, and sliced ½ inch (12 mm) thick (about 5 cups)

2 tablespoons fresh lemon juice, strained

¾ cup (6 oz/185 g) firmly packed light or dark brown sugar

2 tablespoons cornstarch (cornflour)

1 teaspoon ground cinnamon

½ teaspoon freshly grated nutmeg

¼ teaspoon salt

2 tablespoons cold unsalted butter, cut into small pieces

1 tablespoon granulated sugar

Sweetened Whipped Cream (page 111) or vanilla ice cream for serving (optional)

HOLIDAY PIES

As the autumn and winter holidays approach, so do chilly days and long nights—the perfect time for enjoying the welcoming warmth and spicy aromas that fill your kitchen when you bake a pie. Whether you choose a traditional apple or pumpkin pie or an elegant tart made with cranberries and caramel, these are the quintessential desserts that make holiday celebrations complete.

CINNAMON APPLE CRUMB PIE
44

SPICED PUMPKIN PIE
47

CRANBERRY CHESS PIE
48

MOCK MINCEMEAT PIE
51

SWEET POTATO PIE WITH PECAN STREUSEL
52

CARAMEL CRANBERRY-ALMOND TART
55

CHOCOLATE SILK PIE
56

CINNAMON APPLE CRUMB PIE

Fold the dough round in half and carefully transfer to a 9-inch (23-cm) pie pan or dish. Unfold and ease the round into the pan, without stretching it, and pat it firmly into the bottom and up the sides of the pan. Using kitchen scissors, trim the edge of the dough round, leaving ¾ inch (2 cm) of overhang. Fold the overhang under itself and pinch it together to create a high edge on the pan's rim. Flute the edge decoratively (page 107).

To make the crumb topping, in a small bowl, stir together the flour, brown sugar, cinnamon, and salt. Using a pastry blender, cut in the butter until the mixture is crumbly. Cover and chill in the refrigerator until ready to use.

To make the filling, place the apples in a large bowl, sprinkle with the lemon juice, and toss to coat evenly. In a small bowl, stir together the granulated sugar, cornstarch, cinnamon, nutmeg, cloves, and salt. Sprinkle the sugar mixture over the apples and toss to distribute evenly. Immediately transfer to the dough-lined pan. Sprinkle evenly with the crumb topping.

Refrigerate the pie until the dough is firm, 20–30 minutes. Meanwhile, place an oven rack in the lower third of the oven and preheat to 375°F (190°C).

Bake the pie until the crust is golden and the filling is thick and bubbling, 50–60 minutes. Transfer to a wire rack and let cool completely to set. Serve at room temperature or rewarm in a 350°F (180°C) oven for 10–15 minutes just before serving.

MAKES ONE 9-INCH (23-CM) PIE, OR 8 SERVINGS

CRUMB TOPPING

A crumb topping is a simple and delicious way to finish a fruit pie, crisp, or crumble. When assembling the topping, be sure the butter is cold so that it can be cut into the flour and other ingredients easily. Once the mixture resembles coarse crumbs, it is ready for sprinkling over the fruit. When baked, the topping will be sweet, crisp, and golden—the perfect complement to the tart and tender apple filling in this recipe. Other pies that could be made with crumb toppings include berry (page 28), peach (page 32), and apricot (page 36).

1 rolled-out Basic Pie Dough round (page 110)

FOR THE CRUMB TOPPING:

½ cup (2½ oz/75 g) unbleached all-purpose (plain) flour

⅓ cup (2½ oz/75 g) firmly packed light or dark brown sugar

1 teaspoon ground cinnamon

¼ teaspoon salt

5 tablespoons (2½ oz/75 g) cold unsalted butter, cut into ¼-inch (6-mm) cubes

FOR THE FILLING:

7 large, tart, firm apples (page 40), peeled, halved lengthwise, cored, and cut into ½-inch (12-mm) dice (about 6 cups)

1 tablespoon fresh lemon juice, strained

⅓ cup (3 oz/90 g) granulated sugar

2 tablespoons cornstarch (cornflour)

1 teaspoon ground cinnamon

½ teaspoon freshly grated nutmeg

¼ teaspoon ground cloves

Pinch of salt

SPICED PUMPKIN PIE

1 rolled-out Basic Pie
Dough round (page 110)

½ cup (3½ oz/105 g)
firmly packed light or
dark brown sugar

2 large eggs

1 teaspoon ground
cinnamon

1 teaspoon ground ginger

½ teaspoon salt

¼ teaspoon ground cloves

¼ teaspoon freshly grated
nutmeg

1 cup (8 oz/250 g) canned
or fresh pumpkin purée
(far right)

1½ cups (12 fl oz/375 ml)
heavy (double) cream

Fold the dough round in half and carefully transfer to a 9-inch
(23-cm) pie pan or dish. Unfold and ease the round into the pan,
without stretching it, and pat it firmly into the bottom and up the
sides of the pan. Using kitchen scissors, trim the edge of the
dough round, leaving ¾ inch (2 cm) of overhang. Fold the overhang
under itself and pinch it together to create a high edge on the
pan's rim. Flute the edge decoratively (page 107).

Refrigerate or freeze the pie shell until firm, about 30 minutes.
Meanwhile, place an oven rack in the lower third of the oven and
preheat to 375°F (190°C).

Partially bake the pie shell as directed on page 109. Transfer to a
wire rack. Place an oven rack in the middle of the oven and reduce
the oven temperature to 350°F (180°C).

In a large bowl, whisk together the brown sugar and eggs until
well blended. Add the cinnamon, ginger, salt, cloves, and nutmeg
and mix well. Add the pumpkin purée and cream and whisk until
smooth. Pour into the partially baked pie shell.

Bake the pie until the filling is slightly risen and firm in the middle,
35–45 minutes. Transfer to a wire rack and let cool. Serve slightly
warm or at room temperature.

*Serving Tip: Serve each wedge with a dollop of Sweetened Whipped
Cream (page 111).*

MAKES ONE 9-INCH (23-CM) PIE. OR 8 SERVINGS

FRESH PUMPKIN PURÉE
To make fresh purée, first find
a good baking pumpkin, such
as Sugar Pie, Baby Bear, or
Cheese. Split the pumpkin in
half, leaving the seeds in place,
and put the halves, cut sides
down, in a baking dish. Add
water to a depth of ½ inch
(12 mm). Bake at 350°F (180°C)
until a knife easily pierces the
pumpkin, about 45 minutes,
adding water as needed
to maintain the original level.
When the pumpkin is cool,
scoop out and discard the
seeds, then scoop out the
flesh. Purée the flesh in a food
processor or blender until
smooth. The purée freezes
well for up to 3 months.

CRANBERRY CHESS PIE

Fold the dough round in half and carefully transfer to a 9-inch (23-cm) pie pan or dish. Unfold and ease the round into the pan, without stretching it, and pat it firmly into the bottom and up the sides of the pan. Using kitchen scissors, trim the edge of the dough round, leaving ¾ inch (2 cm) of overhang. Fold the overhang under itself and pinch it together to create a high edge on the pan's rim. Using a small, sharp knife, make slices around the edge of the crust, leaving about 1 inch (2.5 cm) between each slice. Fold every other slice up toward the center of the pie to create a decorative chessboard edge.

Refrigerate or freeze the pie shell until firm, about 30 minutes. Meanwhile, place an oven rack in the lower third of the oven and preheat to 375°F (190°C).

Partially bake the pie shell as directed on page 109. Transfer to a wire rack. Leave the oven rack in place and leave the oven temperature at 375°F (190°C).

In a bowl, whisk together the sugar, melted butter, and salt. Add the eggs one at a time, beating until smooth after each addition. Stir in the flour, then the buttermilk, vinegar, and orange zest, mixing well. Stir in the cranberries. Scrape the mixture into the partially baked pie shell.

Bake the pie until the top is lightly golden brown and domed and the filling is firm, 50–60 minutes. Transfer to a wire rack and let cool completely. Serve at room temperature.

MAKES ONE 9-INCH (23-CM) PIE, OR 8 SERVINGS

CHESS PIE

With its simple custardlike filling of eggs, sugar, butter, and a little flour, chess pie is a classic dessert of the American South. A number of theories exist on the origin of the name. One considers it a variation on the word *cheese*, which came about because early cookbooks referred to pies with custard fillings as cheesecakes due to their curdlike texture. Another claims it is the result of its resemblance to an old-fashioned tart from Chester, England. Yet another insists that it comes from the fact that the pie kept well in the traditional storage cabinet known as a pie chest.

1 rolled-out Basic Pie Dough round (page 110)

1⅓ cups (11 oz/345 g) sugar

½ cup (4 oz/125 g) unsalted butter, melted

⅛ teaspoon salt

3 large eggs

¼ cup (1½ oz/45 g) unbleached all-purpose (plain) flour

⅓ cup (3 fl oz/80 ml) buttermilk

1 teaspoon cider vinegar

2 teaspoons finely grated orange zest

2 cups (8 oz/250 g) fresh or frozen cranberries, coarsely chopped

MOCK MINCEMEAT PIE

2 rolled-out Basic Pie
Dough rounds (page 110)

½ cup (3 oz/90 g) dark
raisins or dried currants

½ cup (3 oz/90 g) golden
raisins (sultanas)

½ cup (2 oz/60 g) dried
cranberries

4 large, firm, tart apples
(page 40), peeled, halved
lengthwise, cored, and
quartered

1 teaspoon finely grated
lemon zest

1 teaspoon finely grated
orange zest

¾ cup (6 oz/185 g) firmly
packed light or dark brown
sugar

1 tablespoon cornstarch
(cornflour)

¼ teaspoon ground
allspice

¼ teaspoon ground
cinnamon

¼ teaspoon ground cloves

¼ teaspoon ground ginger

¼ teaspoon freshly grated
nutmeg

¼ cup (2 fl oz/60 ml)
dark rum

Fold 1 dough round in half and carefully transfer to a 9-inch (23-cm) pie pan or dish. Unfold and ease into the pan, patting it firmly into the bottom and up the sides. Using kitchen scissors, trim the edge of the dough round, leaving ¾ inch (2 cm) of overhang. Set the dough-lined pan aside, along with the second dough round, in a cool place until ready to use.

In a food processor, combine the dark raisins, golden raisins, and cranberries and pulse to chop and combine, about 1 minute. Add the apples and pulse to chop into small pieces. Add the lemon and orange zests. Scrape the mixture into a bowl. Add the brown sugar, cornstarch, allspice, cinnamon, cloves, ginger, nutmeg, and rum and mix well. Immediately transfer the mixture to the dough-lined pan.

Fold the reserved dough round in half and carefully position over half of the filled pie. Unfold and trim the edge neatly, leaving 1 inch (2.5 cm) of overhang, then fold the edge of the top round under the edge of the bottom round and crimp the edges to seal (page 10). Gather the dough scraps and roll out about ⅛ inch (3 mm) thick. Using a very small cookie cutter, cut out shapes of dough. Brush the undersides of the dough shapes with cold water and arrange on the top crust. Using a small, sharp knife, cut 5 or 6 holes or slits in the top crust to allow steam to escape.

Refrigerate the pie until the dough is firm, 20–30 minutes. Meanwhile, place an oven rack in the lower third of the oven and preheat to 375°F (190°C).

Bake the pie until the crust is golden and the filling is thick and bubbling, 50–60 minutes. Transfer to a wire rack and let cool completely to set. Serve at room temperature or rewarm in a 350°F (180°C) oven for 10–15 minutes just before serving.

MAKES ONE 9-INCH (23-CM) PIE, OR 8 SERVINGS

MINCEMEAT

In the past, making mincemeat, a mixture of apples, dried fruits, spices, lean meat such as beef or venison, and brandy, rum, or Madeira, was a way to preserve the harvest. It was canned in late summer or early autumn and left to age and mellow until winter, when it would be opened and enjoyed, especially as a filling for Christmas pies. Nowadays, mincemeat is usually made without meat, although some traditionalists in Britain and the United States add suet (beef fat), and/or meat. It also is sometimes made and used immediately, rather than aged.

SWEET POTATO PIE WITH PECAN STREUSEL

SWEET POTATOES

Sweet potatoes are the edible roots of a plant in the morning glory family. Some have tan skin and pale yellow flesh and a dry, fluffy texture when cooked similar to that of a regular potato. Others have dark reddish or purplish skin and deep orange flesh and a soft, moist texture when cooked. The latter are sweeter and are known in the United States as yams, although they are not true yams, which belong to a different species and are rarely available in the United States. Both types of sweet potatoes can be used for this recipe, although the yam, particularly the Garnet yam, is preferred.

Fold the dough round in half and transfer to a 9-inch (23-cm) pie pan or dish. Unfold and ease into the pan, patting it firmly into the bottom and up the sides. Using kitchen scissors, trim the edge of the dough round, leaving ¾ inch (2 cm) of overhang. Fold the overhang under itself and pinch it together to create a high edge on the pan's rim. Flute the edge decoratively (page 107).

Refrigerate or freeze the pie shell until firm, about 30 minutes. Meanwhile, place an oven rack in the lower third of the oven and preheat to 375°F (190°C). Partially bake the pie shell as directed on page 109. Transfer to a wire rack. Leaving the oven rack in place, reduce the oven temperature to 350°F (180°C).

To make the pecan streusel, in a small bowl, stir together the brown sugar, pecans, and cinnamon. Set aside.

To make the filling, prick the yam several times with a fork, put directly on the oven rack, and bake until tender when pierced with a knife, about 55 minutes. Alternatively, cook the yam in the microwave on high heat until tender, about 6 minutes on each side. Set aside to cool. Peel the cooled yam and mash the pulp with a fork, or purée in a food processor, until smooth. Measure out 1 cup (8 oz/250 g) of the purée for the filling. (Reserve any remaining yam for another use.) In a large bowl, stir together the brown sugar, salt, and eggs. Add the cinnamon, ginger, and allspice and mix well. Stir in the yam purée and cream and beat until smooth. Pour into the partially baked pie shell.

Bake until the filling is firm, about 20 minutes. Remove the pie from the oven, quickly sprinkle the pecan streusel evenly over the surface, and then continue to bake until the filling is slightly risen and firm in the middle, 20–25 minutes longer. Slice into wedges and serve with whipped cream.

MAKES ONE 9-INCH (23-CM) PIE, OR 8 SERVINGS

1 rolled-out Basic Pie Dough round (page 110)

FOR THE PECAN STREUSEL:

1 tablespoon firmly packed light brown sugar

¼ cup (1 oz/30 g) pecans, coarsely chopped

¼ teaspoon ground cinnamon

FOR THE FILLING:

1 large Garnet yam (orange-fleshed sweet potato), 12–14 oz (375–440 g)

¾ cup (6 oz/185 g) firmly packed light brown sugar

½ teaspoon salt

2 large eggs

1 teaspoon ground cinnamon

1 teaspoon ground ginger

¼ teaspoon ground allspice

1¼ cups (10 fl oz/310 ml) heavy (double) cream

Sweetened Whipped Cream (page 111) for serving

CARAMEL CRANBERRY-ALMOND TART

1 rolled-out Basic Tart
Dough round (page 111)

1 cup (8 oz/250 g) sugar

2 tablespoons water

1 cup (8 fl oz/250 ml)
heavy (double) cream

1½ cups (6 oz/185 g)
fresh or frozen cranberries

1 cup (4 oz/125 g) sliced
(flaked) almonds, toasted
(page 114)

Fold the dough round in half and carefully transfer to a 9½-inch (24-cm) tart pan, preferably with a removable bottom. Unfold and ease the round into the pan, without stretching it, and pat it firmly into the bottom and up the sides of the pan. Trim off any excess dough by gently running a rolling pin across the top of the pan. Press the dough into the sides to extend it slightly above the rim to offset any shrinkage during baking.

Refrigerate or freeze the tart shell until firm, about 30 minutes. Meanwhile, place an oven rack in the lower third of the oven and preheat to 375°F (190°C). Partially bake the tart shell as directed on page 109. Transfer to a wire rack. Place an oven rack in the middle of the oven and reduce the oven temperature to 325°F (165°C).

In a heavy-bottomed saucepan, stir together the sugar and water. Bring the mixture to a boil over medium heat and continue cooking, shaking or tilting the pan but not stirring (which would cause the sugar to recrystallize), until the sugar dissolves and the syrup begins to turn golden. Reduce the heat to medium-low and continue cooking until the syrup is golden brown, 6–8 minutes. Remove from the heat.

Place a sieve over the top of the saucepan to prevent splattering and slowly pour in the cream; be careful not to let the hot syrup bubble up and splatter. When the bubbling stops, whisk well. Add the cranberries and almonds and stir to combine. Pour the mixture into the partially baked tart shell.

Bake the tart until the cranberries have collapsed and the mixture is bubbling, 25–30 minutes. Transfer to a wire rack and let cool completely. If using a tart pan with a removable bottom, let the sides fall away (page 105), then slide the tart onto a serving plate. Serve at room temperature.

MAKES ONE 9½-INCH (24-CM) TART, OR 8 SERVINGS

CARAMEL SYRUP

For this pie, sugar and water are cooked into a thick, caramelized syrup. The syrup is extremely hot; do not touch or taste it until it has cooled. Use a light-colored saucepan so you can judge the color of the caramel, and do not allow the syrup to turn dark brown. Removed from the heat, the syrup will thicken quickly; use it as soon as possible. Remelt it over low heat if necessary. Adding a squeeze of lemon juice or 1 tablespoon corn syrup in the beginning will prevent the sugar from recrystallizing and help keep the syrup smooth and clear.

CHOCOLATE SILK PIE

Fold the dough round in half and carefully transfer to a 9-inch (23-cm) pie pan or dish. Unfold and ease the round into the pan, without stretching it, and pat it firmly into the bottom and up the sides of the pan. Using kitchen scissors, trim the edge of the dough round, leaving ¾ inch (2 cm) of overhang. Fold the overhang under itself and pinch it together to create a high edge on the pan's rim. Flute the edge decoratively (page 107).

Refrigerate or freeze the pie shell until firm, about 30 minutes. Meanwhile, place an oven rack in the lower third of the oven and preheat to 375°F (190°C). Fully bake the pie shell as directed on page 109. Transfer to a wire rack and let cool completely.

In the top of a double boiler (page 25), whisk together the eggs and the sugar until pale. Attach a candy thermometer (left) to the side of the top pan and set over, but not touching, simmering water in the bottom pan. Cook, stirring constantly, until the mixture reaches 140°F (60°C). Keep the mixture at 140°–150°F (60°–65°C) for 5 minutes. (If the mixture climbs above 150°F/ 65°C, remove it from the heat.) After 5 minutes, add the slivered chocolate and stir until the chocolate is melted. Remove from the heat and stir in the vanilla and rum. Let cool until warm but not hot, about 10 minutes. Stir the butter pieces into the warm chocolate mixture and mix until smooth. Pour into the fully baked pie shell. Refrigerate until firm, 3–4 hours.

Put the white chocolate in the top of the double boiler. Set over barely simmering water until melted, then stir until smooth. Alternatively, in a bowl, melt the white chocolate in the microwave for 30-second intervals. Using a fork, drizzle the white chocolate in a crosshatch pattern over the chilled pie. Refrigerate the pie until ready to serve, but let sit at room temperature for 20 minutes before serving, to take the chill off.

MAKES ONE 9-INCH (23-CM) PIE, OR 8 SERVINGS

1 rolled-out Basic Pie Dough round (page 110)

5 large eggs

1 cup (8 oz/250 g) sugar

5 oz (155 g) semisweet (plain) chocolate, chopped into thin slivers

2 teaspoons vanilla extract (essence)

1 tablespoon dark rum

1 cup (8 oz/250 g) unsalted butter, cut into pieces, at room temperature

1 chunk (1 oz/30 g) white chocolate

SIMPLE PIES

The recipes in this chapter share both simplicity of flavors and ease of preparation. In fact, many use a cookie-crumb crust rather than a rolled crust, a boon to the busy baker. Although their baking time is limited, keep in mind that these recipes are not instant. They require at least 3 to 4 hours of refrigeration to set, so be sure to prepare them well in advance of serving.

COCONUT CUSTARD PIE

DRIED COCONUT

Dried coconut is sold in two styles, shredded and flaked. Either may be used here. Both are nearly always sold sweetened, as called for in this recipe, though it is possible to buy unsweetened dried coconut in health-food stores and some supermarkets. Look for dried coconut in plastic bags or cans (the latter is moister) on market shelves. Once the container has been opened, refrigerate the coconut. Toasting the coconut will bring out its naturally nutty flavor.

Fold the dough round in half and carefully transfer to a 9-inch (23-cm) pie pan or dish. Unfold and ease the round into the pan, without stretching it, and pat it firmly into the bottom and up the sides of the pan. Using kitchen scissors, trim the edge of the dough round, leaving ¾ inch (2 cm) of overhang. Fold the overhang under itself and pinch it together to create a high edge on the pan's rim. Flute the edge decoratively (page 107).

Refrigerate or freeze the pie shell until firm, about 30 minutes. Meanwhile, place an oven rack in the lower third of the oven and preheat to 375°F (190°C).

Partially bake the pie shell as directed on page 109. Transfer to a wire rack. Place an oven rack in the middle of the oven, and reduce the oven temperature to 350°F (180°C).

Spread the coconut evenly on a baking sheet and bake until lightly golden, about 12 minutes. Pour onto a plate to cool.

In a bowl, whisk together the eggs, sugar, and salt until blended. Add the flour, milk, melted butter, and lemon juice and zest and mix well. Stir in the toasted coconut and mix to combine. Pour the mixture into the partially baked crust.

Bake the pie until the top is golden and the filling is firm in the center, 45–55 minutes. Transfer to a wire rack and let cool completely. Serve at room temperature.

MAKES ONE 9-INCH (23-CM) PIE. OR 8 SERVINGS

1 rolled-out Basic Pie Dough round (page 110)

1½ cups (6 oz/185 g) sweetened shredded or flaked dried coconut

3 large eggs

1 cup (8 oz/250 g) sugar

¼ teaspoon salt

2 tablespoons unbleached all-purpose (plain) flour

1 cup (8 fl oz/250 ml) whole milk

1 tablespoon unsalted butter, melted

2 teaspoons fresh lemon juice, strained

1 teaspoon finely grated lemon zest

CITRUS CHIFFON PIE

¼ cup (2 fl oz/60 ml) cold water

2¼ teaspoons (1 package) unflavored powdered gelatin

¾ cup (6 oz/185 g) granulated sugar

⅛ teaspoon salt

¾ cup (6 fl oz/180 ml) fresh lemon juice, strained

1 tablespoon finely grated orange zest

4 large egg yolks, lightly beaten

1¼ cups (10 fl oz/310 ml) heavy (double) cream

¼ cup (1 oz/30 g) confectioners' (icing) sugar

1 Cookie Crumb Crust (page 110), made with gingersnaps

Have ready an ice bath made by partially filling a large bowl with cold water and ice cubes.

Pour the ¼ cup cold water into a saucepan and sprinkle with the gelatin. Let sit until the gelatin softens and swells, 5–10 minutes. Stir in the granulated sugar, salt, lemon juice, orange zest, and egg yolks; the gelatin will be lumpy. Place the gelatin mixture over medium heat and cook, stirring continuously, until the gelatin melts and the mixture thickens, 6–8 minutes. Do not allow the mixture to boil. Set the saucepan in the ice bath and let cool until the mixture is cold to the touch.

In a large bowl, using an electric mixer on medium-high speed or a whisk, whip together the cream and confectioners' sugar until thick, soft peaks form. Spoon the whipped cream into the gelatin mixture and fold together with a rubber spatula until smooth. Pour into the prepared crumb crust, smoothing the top with a rubber spatula.

Refrigerate the pie until it is cold and firm, 3–4 hours, but let sit at room temperature for 20 minutes before serving, to take the chill off.

Note: This recipe contains eggs that may be only partially cooked; for more information, see page 113.

MAKES ONE 9-INCH (23-CM) PIE, OR 8 SERVINGS

GELATIN

Gelatin is an odorless, colorless, tasteless thickener derived from collagen, a protein extracted from the bones, cartilage, and tendons of animals. There are two forms of gelatin available: powdered gelatin, popular with American cooks, and sheet or leaf gelatin, which is commonly used in Europe. Both need to be hydrated and melted before they can be added to a recipe. Do not confuse powdered gelatin with the sweetened, fruit-flavored gelatin desserts sold in boxes.

CHOCOLATE PUDDING PIE

CHOCOLATE CURLS

To make decorative chocolate curls, wrap a medium-sized chunk of semisweet (plain) chocolate in plastic wrap. Rub the wrapped chocolate between your hands for 1 or 2 minutes to warm it; the chocolate should not melt. For larger chunks, microwave on low for about 5 seconds. Unwrap the chocolate and, using a vegetable peeler, slowly and evenly scrape the edge of the chunk until curls form. If the chocolate is cold, the peeler will make ragged shavings rather than curls, so repeat warming the chocolate as necessary. Refrigerate the curls until ready to use.

To make the filling, in a heavy nonaluminum saucepan over low heat, warm together the milk and chocolate, whisking until the chocolate is melted; the mixture will be speckled.

In a bowl, whisk together the egg yolks and sugar until pale yellow. Add the cornstarch and salt, then the vanilla, and beat well. Slowly pour the warm chocolate mixture into the yolk mixture, mixing well. Return the mixture to the saucepan and cook over medium heat until it thickens and begins to bubble slowly, 6–8 minutes. Remove from the heat and stir until smooth, about 1 minute.

Pour the filling into the crumb crust and smooth with a spatula. Cover with plastic wrap, pressing it directly onto the surface, and refrigerate until completely cold and firm, 2–3 hours.

To make the topping, using an electric mixer on medium-high speed or a whisk, whip together the cream, sugar, and vanilla until stiff peaks form. Spread the cream on top of the pie. Decorate with chocolate curls. Refrigerate until ready to serve, but let sit at room temperature for 20 minutes before serving, to take the chill off.

MAKES ONE 9-INCH (23-CM) PIE, OR 8 SERVINGS

FOR THE FILLING:

2½ cups (20 fl oz/625 ml) whole milk

5 oz (155 g) semisweet (plain) chocolate, chopped into slivers

4 large egg yolks

¾ cup (6 oz/185 g) sugar

3 tablespoons cornstarch (cornflour)

¼ teaspoon salt

1½ teaspoons vanilla extract (essence)

1 Cookie Crumb Crust (page 110), made from chocolate cookies

FOR THE TOPPING:

1 cup (8 fl oz/250 ml) heavy (double) cream

1 tablespoon sugar

1 teaspoon vanilla extract (essence)

Chocolate curls for serving (far left)

CREAM CHEESE PIE WITH ORANGES

4 or 5 navel oranges,
2–2½ lb (1–1.25 kg) total
weight

½ lb (250 g) cream cheese,
at room temperature
(see Note)

1 can (14 fl oz/430 ml)
sweetened condensed
milk

1 teaspoon vanilla extract
(essence)

⅓ cup (3 fl oz/80 ml) fresh
lemon juice, strained

1 Cookie Crumb Crust
(page 110), made with
graham crackers, ginger-
snaps, or chocolate
cookies

Zest 1 of the oranges (page 31) to measure 1 teaspoon finely grated zest. Set aside. Using a sharp knife, peel all of the oranges *(right)*. Slice the oranges crosswise into thin rounds and set aside on a paper towel to drain.

In a bowl, using an electric mixer on medium speed, beat the cream cheese until smooth. Add the condensed milk, reserved orange zest, and vanilla and beat until smooth. Stir in the lemon juice. Pour the mixture into the prepared crumb crust and smooth the top. Arrange the orange slices, overlapping them, in a decorative pattern on top of the pie, covering the filling completely.

Refrigerate the pie until chilled, about 1 hour, but let sit at room temperature for 20 minutes before serving, to take the chill off.

Note: Do not use nonfat cream cheese for this recipe. Cream cheese with one-third less fat will work, but traditional full-fat cream cheese will yield the best results.

MAKES ONE 9-INCH (23-CM) PIE, OR 8 SERVINGS

PEELING CITRUS

To peel a citrus fruit so that it can be thinly sliced, start by cutting a thick slice off both bottom and top, exposing the flesh beneath the peel. Then, steadying the fruit upright on a cutting board, slice off the peel in thick strips, following the contour of the fruit and cutting off the white pith and membrane with the peel, again revealing the flesh. If a recipe calls for sectioning, rather than slicing, the fruit, hold the fully peeled fruit in one hand and carefully cut along either side of each section, freeing it from the membrane.

LEMON CREAM TART

Fold the dough round in half and carefully transfer to a 9½-inch (24-cm) tart pan, preferably with a removable bottom. Unfold and ease the round into the pan, without stretching it, and pat it firmly into the bottom and up the sides of the pan. Trim off any excess dough by gently running a rolling pin across the top of the pan. Press the dough into the sides to extend it slightly above the rim to offset any shrinkage during baking.

Refrigerate or freeze the tart shell until firm, about 30 minutes. Meanwhile, place an oven rack in the lower third of the oven and preheat to 375°F (190°C).

Fully bake the tart shell as directed on page 109. Transfer to a wire rack and let cool completely. Leaving the oven rack in place, reduce the oven temperature to 350°F (180°C).

In a bowl, using an electric mixer on medium speed, beat together the egg yolks and lemon zest until well mixed, about 1 minute. Add the condensed milk, lemon juice, and salt, beating well after each addition. Pour into the fully baked tart shell.

Bake the tart until the filling is firm in the center, 12–14 minutes. Transfer to a wire rack and let cool completely until set, 1–2 hours. If using a tart pan with a removable bottom, let the sides fall away (page 105), then slide the tart onto a serving plate. Cut into wedges and serve with a dollop of whipped cream, if using.

MAKES ONE 9½-INCH (24-CM) TART, OR 8 SERVINGS

1 rolled-out Basic Tart Dough round (page 111)

4 large egg yolks

4 teaspoons finely grated lemon zest

1 can (14 fl oz/430 ml) sweetened condensed milk

½ cup (4 fl oz/125 ml) fresh lemon juice, strained

Pinch of salt

Sweetened Whipped Cream (page 111) for serving (optional)

RASPBERRY CREAM PIE

FOR THE FILLING:

¼ cup (2 fl oz/60 ml) cold water

1½ teaspoons unflavored powdered gelatin

⅔ cup (5 fl oz/160 ml) fresh raspberry purée *(far right),* at room temperature

2 large eggs

½ cup (4 oz/125 g) sugar

Pinch of salt

¾ cup (6 fl oz/180 ml) heavy (double) cream

1 Cookie Crumb Crust (page 110), made with chocolate cookies or gingersnaps

Sweetened Whipped Cream (page 111) for serving

Whole fresh raspberries for serving

To make the filling, pour the cold water into a saucepan and sprinkle with the gelatin. Let sit until the gelatin softens and swells, 5–10 minutes. Heat the gelatin over medium heat until clear and fluid, stirring as needed to dissolve, 3–4 minutes. Stir the gelatin mixture into the raspberry purée.

In a bowl, using an electric mixer on medium-high speed or a whisk, whip together the eggs, sugar, and salt until pale yellow. In a large bowl, using the mixer on medium-high speed or a whisk, whip the cream until thick, soft peaks form. Add the egg mixture and raspberry purée to the whipped cream and whip until smooth. Pour into the crumb crust, smoothing the top with a rubber spatula.

Refrigerate until the filling is cold and firm, 4–6 hours.

Let the pie sit at room temperature for 20 minutes before serving, to take the chill off. Slice into wedges and serve with dollops of whipped cream and fresh raspberries alongside.

Note: This recipe contains raw eggs; for more information, see page 113.

MAKES ONE 9-INCH (23-CM) PIE, OR 8 SERVINGS

FRESH RASPBERRY PURÉE
Gently rinse and dry 4 cups (1 lb/500 g) raspberries. Place the berries in a food processor or blender and purée until smooth. Pour the purée through a medium-mesh sieve placed over a bowl to remove the seeds. You can also use another berry for this purée; other varieties that would work include blackberry, boysenberry, olallieberry, and loganberry.

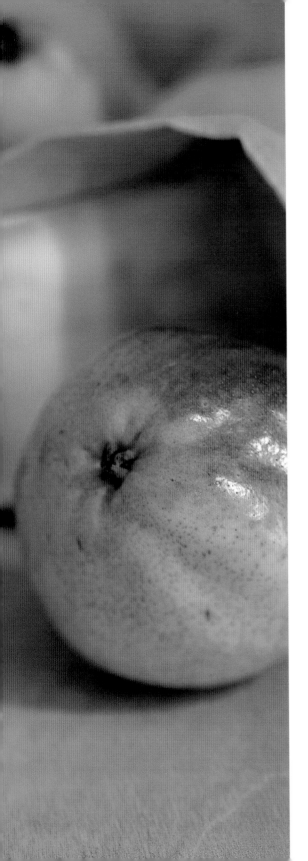

ELEGANT TARTS

Tarts, with their buttery crusts and fluted edges, have long been a favorite in European kitchens. Without a top crust to hide their fillings, they make an elegant impression with spirals of thinly sliced fruits or smooth layers of satiny chocolate or sweet lemon curd. Serve a narrow slice of tart or an individual tartlet for a stylish finish to any occasion.

ITALIAN ALMOND TART
74

CRÈME BRÛLÉE TARTLETS
77

LEMON CURD TART
78

FRESH MINT–CHOCOLATE TRUFFLE TART
81

PEAR AND FRANGIPANE TART
82

RASPBERRY AND CHOCOLATE TARTLETS
85

STRAWBERRY TART WITH ORANGE CREAM
86

ITALIAN ALMOND TART

Fold the dough round in half and carefully transfer to a 9½-inch (24-cm) tart pan, preferably with a removable bottom. Unfold and ease the round into the pan, without stretching it, and pat it firmly into the bottom and up the sides of the pan. Trim off any excess dough by gently running a rolling pin across the top of the pan. Press the dough into the sides to extend it slightly above the rim to offset any shrinkage during baking.

Refrigerate or freeze the tart shell until firm, about 30 minutes. Meanwhile, place an oven rack in the lower third of the oven and preheat to 375°F (190°C).

Partially bake the tart shell as directed on page 109. Transfer to a wire rack. Place an oven rack in the middle of the oven, and reduce the oven temperature to 350°F (180°C).

In a bowl, using an electric mixer on medium speed or a whisk, beat the butter until smooth. Add the almond paste, one piece at a time, beating until smooth after each addition. While continuing to beat, sprinkle in the sugar. Add the eggs one at a time, mixing well after each addition. Stir in the flour.

Spread the jam evenly in the bottom of the partially baked tart shell. Spoon in the almond paste mixture and spread evenly over the jam. Sprinkle the surface evenly with the sliced almonds.

Bake the tart until the filling is golden and the middle is firm to the touch, 35–45 minutes. Transfer to a wire rack and let the tart cool completely. If using a tart pan with a removable bottom, let the sides fall away (page 105), then slide the tart onto a serving plate. Serve at room temperature.

MAKES ONE 9½-INCH (24-CM) TART, OR 8 SERVINGS

1 rolled-out Basic Tart Dough round (page 111)

½ cup (4 oz/125 g) unsalted butter, at room temperature

½ lb (250 g) almond paste, cut into 1-inch (2.5-cm) cubes

¼ cup (2 oz/60 g) sugar

2 large eggs

⅓ cup (2 oz/60 g) unbleached all-purpose (plain) flour

⅓ cup (3½ oz/105 g) raspberry, plum, or cherry jam

⅓ cup (1½ oz/45 g) sliced (flaked) almonds

CRÈME BRÛLÉE TARTLETS

1 rolled-out Basic Tart Dough round (page 111)

2 cups (16 fl oz/500 ml) heavy (double) cream

½ vanilla bean, split lengthwise

2 large whole eggs, plus 2 large egg yolks

⅓ cup (3 oz/90 g) granulated sugar

⅛ teaspoon salt

¼ cup (2 oz/60 g) turbinado sugar, finely ground in a food processor

Using a 6-inch (15-cm) cardboard circle and a small, sharp knife, cut out 3 or 4 rounds from the tart dough. Press the dough scraps together and reroll to cut out additional rounds. You should have a total of 6. Transfer the rounds to six 4-inch (10-cm) tartlet pans, preferably with removable bottoms. Ease into the pans and pat firmly into the bottoms and up the sides. Trim off any excess dough. Press the dough into the sides to extend it slightly above the rims.

Refrigerate or freeze the tartlet shells until firm, about 30 minutes. Meanwhile, place an oven rack in the lower third of the oven and preheat to 375°F (190°C). Place the tartlets on a baking sheet. Fully bake as directed on page 109. Transfer to a wire rack and let cool.

In a saucepan over medium heat, warm the cream until hot to the touch, 6–8 minutes. Scrape the seeds from the vanilla bean into the cream, then add the pods. In a bowl, whisk together the whole eggs, egg yolks, granulated sugar, and salt until pale yellow. Add 1 cup (8 fl oz/250 ml) of the hot cream while stirring constantly. Mix in the remaining hot cream. Return to the saucepan over medium heat and cook, whisking constantly, until the custard is thick enough to heavily coat the back of a wooden spoon, 4–5 minutes. Strain through a medium-mesh sieve placed over a measuring pitcher. Pour into the tart shells, dividing evenly. Refrigerate until well chilled, 3–4 hours.

Just before serving, preheat the broiler (grill). Sprinkle each tart with 2 teaspoons of the turbinado sugar. One at a time, slip the tarts under the broiler 2–3 inches (5–7.5 cm) from the heat source. Broil (grill) until the sugar caramelizes, 1–2 minutes. Alternatively, use a small kitchen blowtorch to caramelize the sugar. Transfer to a wire rack and let cool for 10 minutes. If using pans with removable bottoms, let the sides fall away (page 105), then slide the tartlets onto individual plates. Serve at once.

MAKES SIX 4-INCH (10-CM) TARTLETS, OR 6 SERVINGS

SUGAR TYPES

Turbinado and Demerara sugars are large, pale brown crystals of pure cane sugar. Turbinado is a washed raw cane sugar with a delicate molasses flavor. Demerara is a type of raw cane sugar specifically from the Demerara area of Guyana in South America. Both of these sugars have a mild brown-sugar flavor and good melting qualities, making them ideal for caramelizing the tops of these tarts. Finely grinding the sugar will yield tarts with a smooth, glasslike top. For a more granular finish, use the sugar in its crystal form. If unavailable, substitute with granulated sugar.

LEMON CURD TART

Fold the dough round in half and carefully transfer to a 9½-inch (24-cm) tart pan, preferably with a removable bottom. Unfold and ease the round into the pan, without stretching it, and pat it firmly into the bottom and up the sides of the pan. Trim off any excess dough by gently running a rolling pin across the top of the pan. Press the dough into the sides to extend it slightly above the rim to offset any shrinkage during baking.

Refrigerate or freeze the tart shell until firm, about 30 minutes. Meanwhile, place an oven rack in the lower third of the oven and preheat to 375°F (190°C).

Fully bake the tart shell as directed on page 109. Transfer to a wire rack and let cool completely.

In a nonaluminum saucepan over medium heat, combine the eggs, egg yolks, sugar, lemon juice, lemon zest, and butter. Cook slowly, stirring constantly with a heatproof rubber spatula, until the butter melts and the mixture is thick enough to coat the back of the spatula and leaves a clear trail when a finger is drawn through it, 7–8 minutes. Remove from the heat and strain through a coarse-mesh sieve placed over a bowl.

Spread the curd evenly in the fully baked tart shell and refrigerate until chilled, 2–3 hours. Using a pastry bag fitted with a small star tip, pipe whipped cream around the edge of the tart (page 111). If using a tart pan with a removable bottom, let the sides fall away (page 105), then slide the tart onto a serving plate. Let sit at room temperature for 20 minutes before serving, to take the chill off.

MAKES ONE 9½-INCH (24-CM) TART, OR 8 SERVINGS

REACTIVE METALS

Acidic ingredients, such as citrus juice, tomatoes, vinegar, wine, and many vegetables, will react with certain metals, including aluminum or cast iron. Although the reaction is harmless, it may turn a mixture gray or leave behind a metallic aftertaste. The same reaction occurs when eggs are cooked in aluminum or cast-iron pans.

For these reasons, recipes that include these ingredients, such as lemon curd and pastry cream, call for the use of nonaluminum pans. Stainless-steel and enamel-lined pans are excellent choices.

1 rolled-out Basic Tart Dough round (page 111)

3 large whole eggs, plus 3 large egg yolks, lightly beaten

¾ cup (6 oz/185 g) sugar

¾ cup (6 fl oz/180 ml) fresh lemon juice, strained (about 6 large lemons)

2 tablespoons finely grated lemon zest

¾ cup (6 oz/185 g) unsalted butter, cut into ¼-inch (6-mm) cubes

Sweetened Whipped Cream (page 111)

FRESH MINT–CHOCOLATE TRUFFLE TART

1 rolled-out Basic Tart Dough rectangle (page 111)

1½ cups (12 fl oz/375 ml) heavy (double) cream

8–10 fresh mint sprigs (about 40 leaves), plus sprigs for garnish

12 oz (375 g) semisweet (plain) chocolate, chopped into small slivers

2 tablespoons light corn syrup

Confectioners' (icing) sugar or unsweetened cocoa powder for dusting

Fold the dough rectangle in half and transfer to a 13¾-by-4¼-inch (35-by-11-cm) tart pan, preferably with a removable bottom. Unfold and ease the rectangle into the pan, without stretching it, and pat it firmly into the bottom and up the sides of the pan. Trim off any excess dough by gently running a rolling pin across the top of the pan. Press the dough into the sides to extend it slightly above the rim to offset any shrinkage during baking.

Refrigerate or freeze the tart shell until firm, about 30 minutes. Meanwhile, place an oven rack in the lower third of the oven and preheat to 375°F (190°C). Fully bake the tart shell as directed on page 109. Transfer to a wire rack and let cool completely.

In a small saucepan over medium heat, warm the cream until small bubbles appear on the surface. Remove from the heat and add the mint sprigs. Let stand for 20–30 minutes.

Put the chocolate in the top of a double boiler (page 25) and set over, but not touching, barely simmering water and melt, stirring occasionally. Alternatively, in a heatproof bowl, melt the chocolate in the microwave for 30-second intervals. Pour the cream through a fine-mesh sieve into the melted chocolate, discarding the mint sprigs. Add the corn syrup and stir until smooth. Pour the filling into the tart shell.

Refrigerate until well chilled, about 1 hour. If using a tart pan with a removable bottom, let the sides fall away (page 105), then slide the tart onto a serving plate. Let sit at room temperature for 20 minutes before serving, to take the chill off. Just before serving, lay strips of waxed paper over the top of the tart and dust lightly with confectioners' sugar *(right)*. Carefully remove the strips and garnish with fresh mint sprigs.

MAKES ONE 13¾-BY-4¼-INCH (35-BY-11-CM) TART, OR 8 SERVINGS

DECORATING WITH SUGAR AND COCOA

Using strips of waxed paper or a stencil when dusting a pie or tart with confectioners' sugar or cocoa powder is a simple and elegant way to add a decorative finish. For rectangular tarts, cut strips of waxed paper. For round pies or tarts, use a precut cake stencil, or cut your own design out of card stock. Lay the strips or stencil over the pie or tart. Put about 1 tablespoon confectioners' (icing) sugar or cocoa powder in a fine-mesh sieve, then tap to sprinkle evenly. Lift off the strips or stencil, leaving the sugar or cocoa pattern behind.

PEAR AND FRANGIPANE TART

Fold the dough round in half and carefully transfer to a 9½-inch (24-cm) tart pan, preferably with a removable bottom. Unfold and ease into the pan and pat it firmly into the bottom and up the sides of the pan. Trim off any excess dough. Press the dough into the sides to extend it slightly above the rim.

Refrigerate or freeze the tart shell until firm, about 30 minutes. Meanwhile, place an oven rack in the lower third of the oven and preheat to 375°F (190°C). Partially bake the tart shell as directed on page 109. Transfer to a wire rack. Leaving the oven temperature at 375°F (190°C), place an oven rack in the middle of the oven.

In a small saucepan over medium heat, melt the butter and cook until golden brown, about 5 minutes. Remove from the heat and let cool to the touch. In a bowl, stir together the ground almonds, sugar, eggs, almond and vanilla extracts, rum, salt, lemon zest, and melted butter. Spread evenly in the tart shell. Slice each pear quarter crosswise into slices ⅛ inch (3 mm) thick, keeping each one together. Arrange each quarter core side down and stem end toward the center in the pan. Use your hand to flatten and fan each quarter slightly and press the slices into the filling.

Bake the tart until the filling is firm to the touch in the center and slightly golden, 40–45 minutes. Transfer to a wire rack to cool. In a saucepan over low heat, heat the jam until it liquefies. Pour through a fine-mesh sieve set over a small bowl. Using a pastry brush, gently brush the top of the tart with a thin coating of jam. If using a tart pan with a removable bottom, let the sides fall away (page 105), then slide the tart onto a serving plate. Serve warm or at room temperature.

Note: The term frangipane *refers to pastry cream or custard made with ground almonds.*

MAKES ONE 9½-INCH (24-CM) TART, OR 8 SERVINGS

PEARS

The best pear varieties to use for baking are Anjou and Bartlett because their texture remains firm and smooth. Anjou pears are almost egg shaped, with green skin that often has a yellow tinge when ripe. Bartlett pears, also known as Williams' pears, have thin skins that ripen from dark green to light green and then to yellow. When choosing pears for baking, select those that are firm but not rock-hard, have a good fragrance, and are smooth and unblemished with their stems still attached. Autumn is the best season for these pears, but they are available almost all year long.

---

1 rolled-out Basic Tart Dough round (page 111)

2 tablespoons unsalted butter

1½ cups (8 oz/250 g) raw unblanched, whole almonds, finely ground (page 114)

⅔ cup (5 oz/155 g) sugar

2 large eggs, lightly beaten

½ teaspoon almond extract (essence)

1 teaspoon vanilla extract (essence)

2 tablespoons dark rum

¼ teaspoon salt

1 teaspoon finely grated fresh lemon zest

2 Anjou or Bartlett (Williams') pears, peeled, quartered, and cored

⅓ cup (3½ oz/105 g) apricot jam

RASPBERRY AND CHOCOLATE TARTLETS

1 rolled-out Basic Tart Dough round (page 111)

8 oz (250 g) semisweet (plain) chocolate, chopped into small slivers

6 tablespoons (3 oz/90 g) unsalted butter

2 tablespoons light corn syrup

¼ cup (2½ oz/75 g) raspberry jam

4 cups (1 lb/500 g) raspberries

Using a 2½- to 3-inch (6- to 7.5-cm) round cookie cutter or a cardboard circle and a small, sharp knife, cut out as many rounds as possible from the tart dough. Press the dough scraps together and reroll to cut out additional rounds. You should have a total of 12. Transfer the rounds to twelve 2-inch (5-cm) tartlet pans. Ease into the pans and pat firmly into the bottoms and up the sides. Trim off any excess dough. Press the dough into the sides to extend it slightly above the rims.

Refrigerate or freeze the tartlet shells until firm, about 30 minutes. Meanwhile, place an oven rack in the lower third of the oven and preheat to 375°F (190°C). Place the tartlet shells on a baking sheet for easy removal from the oven. Fully bake the shells as directed on page 109. Transfer to wire racks and let cool completely.

In the top of a double boiler (page 25), combine the chocolate, butter, and corn syrup. Set over, not touching, barely simmering water and melt, stirring occasionally. Alternatively, in a microwaveproof bowl, combine the chocolate, butter, and corn syrup and melt in the microwave for 30-second intervals. Remove from the stove top or microwave oven and stir until smooth.

Pass the raspberry jam through a medium-mesh sieve to remove the seeds. Spread 1 teaspoon of the jam in the bottom of each shell and fill as full as possible with the chocolate mixture. Let the filled tartlets stand at room temperature until set, 1–2 hours.

Before serving the tartlets, place 1 raspberry, stem end down, on top of the chocolate in the middle of each tartlet and surround with additional raspberries. (You will need 7 or 8 raspberries for each tartlet.) Remove the tartlets from the pans and serve.

MAKES TWELVE SMALL TARTLETS, OR 6 SERVINGS

MELTING CHOCOLATE

You can melt chocolate in a double boiler or in a microwave. If using a double boiler, be sure the water in the bottom pan does not touch the base of the top pan and that it never boils. Any moisture—including steam—that comes in contact with the chocolate could cause it to seize into a lumpy mass. (To save seized chocolate, whisk in vegetable oil or solid vegetable shortening, 1 teaspoon at time, until smooth.) If microwaving the chocolate, check it every 30 seconds to avoid scorching. When the chocolate is shiny and soft, remove it and stir until smooth.

STRAWBERRY TART WITH ORANGE CREAM

COINTREAU

Cointreau is a well-known liqueur from western France, where it was first made more than a century and a half ago in the city of Angers. Colorless and with a strong, pleasing aroma, it has an exotic flavor that is a marriage of sweet orange peels from Spain and bitter orange peels from the Caribbean island of Curaçao. Although similar to Triple Sec, Cointreau is drier. You will find it sold in a distinctive square bottle with a bright red ribbon. A popular after-dinner liqueur, Cointreau is also often used as a flavoring ingredient, as in this tart recipe.

Fold the dough round in half and carefully transfer to a 9½-inch (24-cm) tart pan, preferably with a removable bottom. Unfold and ease the round into the pan, without stretching it, and pat it firmly into the bottom and up the sides of the pan. Trim off any excess dough by running a rolling pin across the top of the pan. Press the dough into the sides to extend it slightly above the rim to offset any shrinkage during baking.

Refrigerate or freeze the tart shell until firm, about 30 minutes. Meanwhile, place an oven rack in the lower third of the oven and preheat to 375°F (190°C).

Fully bake the tart shell as directed on page 109. Transfer to a wire rack and let cool completely.

In a bowl, using an electric mixer on medium speed, beat together the cream cheese and sugar until smooth. Mix in the orange zest and Cointreau. Spread the cream cheese mixture evenly over the bottom of the tart shell. Arrange the strawberry halves, overlapping them, in concentric circles on top of the cream cheese, completely covering the surface of the tart.

In a small saucepan over low heat, heat the apricot jam until it liquefies. Pour through a fine-mesh sieve set over a small bowl to strain out any fruit chunks. Using a small pastry brush, gently brush the strawberries with a thin coating of the jam to glaze the fruit. Refrigerate until ready to serve, then let sit at room temperature for 20 minutes before serving, to take the chill off. If using a tart pan with a removable bottom, let the sides fall away (page 105), then slide the tart onto a serving plate.

MAKES ONE 9½-INCH (24-CM) TART, OR 8 SERVINGS

1 rolled-out Basic Tart Dough round (page 111)

8 oz (250 g) cream cheese (see Note, page 67), at room temperature

¼ cup (2 oz/60 g) sugar

1 teaspoon finely grated orange zest

2 teaspoons Cointreau or other orange liqueur

2 cups (8 oz/250 g) fresh strawberries, hulled and halved lengthwise

½ cup (5 oz/155 g) apricot jam

RUSTIC TARTS

As exquisite as composed fruit tarts can be, the rustic tart (or galette, as the French call it) is common in the countryside, where home cooks are more practical. These recipes call for simply rolling out a flaky butter crust, folding it over a bounty of ripe, fresh fruit, and then baking until tender and golden. The results are simple and delicious.

BLACKBERRY POCKETS

Using a 4-inch (10-cm) round or scalloped cookie cutter, a 4-inch tart pan turned upside down, or a cardboard circle and a small, sharp knife, cut out 3 or 4 rounds from each dough round. Press the dough scraps together and reroll to cut out additional rounds. You should have a total of 12.

In a bowl, toss together the blackberries, cornstarch, sugar, and salt. Lay 6 dough rounds on a baking sheet lined with parchment (baking) paper. Divide the blackberries evenly among the dough rounds. Using a small pastry brush, dampen the edge of each round with cold water. Lay the remaining dough rounds over the blackberries. Gently press the top of each dough round down over the berries; the edges of the dough rounds will not line up. With the tines of a fork, press the outer edge of the 2 dough rounds together.

Refrigerate the pockets on the baking sheet until the dough is firm, 15–20 minutes. Meanwhile, place an oven rack in the lower third of the oven and preheat to 375°F (190°C).

Bake the pockets until golden brown, 35–40 minutes. Transfer the baking sheet to a wire rack to cool slightly. Serve warm.

Serving Tip: Try serving these pockets for breakfast or as a delicious afternoon snack.

MAKES SIX 4-INCH (10-CM) POCKETS, OR 6 SERVINGS

2 rolled-out Basic Pie Dough rounds (page 110)

2 cups (8 oz/250 g) blackberries

2 tablespoons cornstarch (cornflour)

3 tablespoons sugar

Pinch of salt

PARCHMENT PAPER

Parchment paper, also known as baking paper, is a heavy, moisture-resistant paper used to line baking pans and sheets. It is sold in sheets, rolls, and precut pieces to fit cake pans and can withstand temperatures up to 450°F (230°C). It helps make cleanup easy, as the paper is simply slipped from the pan after use. Other uses include creating packets for cooking fish and vegetables, rolling into cones for piping icing, and placing over a pan of simmering vegetables to keep them immersed in the water. Do not substitute waxed paper for parchment paper.

FRESH FIG GALETTE WITH RICOTTA AND HONEY

1 rolled-out Basic Pie
Dough round (page 110)

1 cup (8 oz/250 g) ricotta
cheese

4 tablespoons (3 oz/90 g)
honey

¼ cup (2 fl oz/60 ml) heavy
(double) cream

2 large egg yolks

2 teaspoons finely grated
orange zest

¼ teaspoon ground
cardamom

Pinch of salt

10–12 ripe black Mission
figs (8 oz/250 g), stemmed
and quartered lengthwise

Place the dough round on a baking sheet lined with parchment (baking) paper. Fold in 1 inch (2.5 cm) of the outer edge of the dough and pleat to form a rim for the galette. Refrigerate the dough until firm, 15–20 minutes. Meanwhile, place an oven rack in the lower third of the oven and preheat to 375°F (190°C).

Remove the galette shell from the refrigerator. Line with a sheet of aluminum foil large enough to cover the edges. Cover the center of the galette with a generous layer of pie weights. Partially bake the shell for 20 minutes, then lift an edge of the foil to check the dough. If it looks wet, continue to bake, checking every 5 minutes, until the dough is pale gold. Remove the weights and foil. The total baking time will be 25–30 minutes.

In a bowl, combine the ricotta, 2 tablespoons of the honey, the cream, and the egg yolks and stir to combine thoroughly. Mix in the orange zest, cardamom, and salt. Spread the mixture evenly over the partially baked galette crust.

Return the galette to the oven and bake until the filling is firm in the center, 15–18 minutes. Transfer the galette, still on the baking sheet, to a wire rack and let cool completely, about 30 minutes.

Arrange the figs, cut sides up and stem ends toward the middle, decoratively over the ricotta filling. Drizzle evenly with the remaining 2 tablespoons honey. Serve at once.

MAKES ONE 9½-INCH (24-CM) GALETTE, OR 8 SERVINGS

FIGS

Fresh figs come in many shapes, colors, and sizes. Well-known varieties include the deep purple, sweet-tasting Mission fig, the amber-skinned Kadota, the green-skinned Adriatic, and the golden Calimyrna, or Smyrna, figs. Black Mission figs are the best choice for this recipe. Figs have two seasons; the first begins in early summer and lasts until midsummer, and the second runs from late summer into autumn. Because they do not ripen off the tree, figs must be picked ripe. Choose plump specimens that are soft to the touch but not wrinkled, mushy, or bruised, and that have firm stems.

HARVEST APPLE GALETTE

**PEELING AND
CORING APPLES**

A small, sharp knife is all you need for peeling an apple, although a vegetable peeler may be easier for novice cooks. Once the apple is peeled, a melon baller is a handy tool for coring. First, cut the peeled apple in half from the top (stem end) to the bottom (blossom end). Press the melon baller into the center of one of the halves and twist it to remove the core. If there is any stem or blossom end remaining, use the melon baller in the same way to remove it.

Place the dough round on a baking sheet lined with parchment (baking) paper.

Thinly slice the apple halves crosswise, keeping each half together. Gently nudge one of the apple halves to flatten it slightly, and lay it cored side down in the middle of the pie dough round. Repeat with the remaining apple halves, arranging them around the center apple half and leaving a 1- to 2-inch (2.5- to 5-cm) border of dough uncovered along the edge. Fold the edge of the dough up and over the apples, pleating the dough loosely all around the edge and leaving the galette open in the center (page 97). Dot the apples with the butter and sprinkle with the sugar.

Measure the circumference of the galette and cut a strip of aluminum foil about 2 inches (5 cm) longer and 3–4 inches (7.5–10 cm) wide. Fold the strip in half lengthwise, place it around the edge of the galette, and secure the ends by folding or pinching them together. (The foil helps keep the dough from unfolding.)

Refrigerate the galette on the baking sheet until the dough is firm, 20–30 minutes. Meanwhile, place an oven rack in the lower third of the oven and preheat to 425°F (220°C).

Bake the galette for 15 minutes. Reduce the oven temperature to 375°F (190°C) and continue baking until golden brown and the apples are tender when pierced with a knife, 30–40 minutes longer.

Transfer the baking sheet to a wire rack and let the galette cool until slightly warm or room temperature before serving.

MAKES ONE 9-INCH (23-CM) GALETTE, OR 8 SERVINGS

1 rolled-out Basic Pie Dough round (page 110)

4 large, firm, tart apples (page 40), peeled, halved lengthwise, and cored

1 tablespoon cold unsalted butter, cut into small pieces

2 tablespoons sugar

LITTLE PLUM GALETTES

2 rolled-out Basic Pie
Dough or Basic Tart Dough
rounds (pages 110–11)

½ cup (4 oz/125 g) sugar

¼ teaspoon ground
cinnamon

2 tablespoons cornstarch
(cornflour)

⅛ teaspoon salt

2 lb (1 kg) plums (page 39),
pitted and cut into small
chunks (about 4 cups)

Using a 6-inch (15-cm) cardboard circle and a small, sharp knife, cut out 3 or 4 rounds from each dough round. Press the dough scraps together and reroll to cut out additional rounds. You should have a total of 8.

Carefully transfer the dough rounds to eight 4-inch (10-cm) metal tartlet pans, preferably with removable bottoms, and arrange on a baking sheet. Do not trim the edges of the dough.

In a small bowl, stir together the sugar, cinnamon, cornstarch, and salt. Place the plums in a large bowl, sprinkle with the sugar mixture, and toss to distribute evenly.

Place ½ cup (3 oz/90 g) of the plum mixture into each dough-lined pan. Fold the edges of the dough up and over the plums, pleating the dough loosely all around the edges and leaving the galettes open in the center.

Refrigerate the galettes on the baking sheet until the dough is firm, 15–20 minutes. Meanwhile, place an oven rack in the lower third of the oven and preheat to 375°F (190°C).

Bake the galettes until the crusts are golden and the juice around the plums has thickened, about 40 minutes.

Transfer the baking sheet to a wire rack and let the galettes cool slightly before serving. If using tart pans with removable bottoms, let the sides fall away (page 105), then slide the galettes onto individual plates.

MAKES EIGHT 4-INCH (10-CM) GALETTES, OR 8 SERVINGS

PLEATING DOUGH

Pleating the edges of a crust over the filling will give a fruit pie or tart a pretty, rustic look. Make sure there is a border of dough hanging over the edge of the pan of at least 1 to 2 inches (2.5 to 5 cm). One inch is enough in the case of these small galettes. Using both hands, lift the edge of the dough up and over the fruit and then fold it underneath itself every inch or two until the entire edge is a series of loose folds. Work quickly so your fingers do not melt the butter in the dough, which will produce a tough crust.

TOSSED FRESH FRUIT TART

Fold the dough round in half and transfer to a 9½-inch (24-cm) tart pan, preferably with a removable bottom. Unfold and ease into the pan, patting it firmly into the bottom and up the sides. Trim off any excess dough. Press the dough into the sides to extend it slightly above the rim. Refrigerate or freeze the tart shell until firm, about 30 minutes. Place an oven rack in the lower third of the oven and preheat to 375°F (190°C). Fully bake the tart shell as directed on page 109. Transfer to a wire rack and let cool.

To make the pastry cream, in a nonaluminum saucepan over medium heat, warm the milk until tiny bubbles appear on the surface, 6–8 minutes. In a bowl, whisk together the egg yolks and sugar. Add the cornstarch and salt. Pour in half of the hot milk while whisking constantly. Whisk in the remaining milk and return to the saucepan. Cook over medium heat, whisking constantly, until the mixture thickens to a firm consistency, 5–8 minutes. Scrape into a bowl. Whisk in the vanilla. Cover with plastic wrap, pressing it directly onto the surface of the pastry cream. Refrigerate for 2–3 hours.

To assemble the tart, stir the pastry cream with a rubber spatula until smooth. Spoon into the bottom of the fully baked tart shell and spread evenly.

In a large bowl, combine the strawberries, red and green grapes, and blueberries. In a small saucepan over low heat, heat the apricot jam until it liquefies. Pour through a fine-mesh sieve set over a small bowl. Pour the warm jam over the fruit and toss gently until the fruit is well coated. Pile the fruit on top of the pastry cream and arrange into a dome. If using a tart pan with a removable bottom, let the sides fall away (page 105), then slide the tart onto a serving plate. Serve at once.

MAKES ONE 9½-INCH (24-CM) TART. OR 8 SERVINGS

STRAWBERRIES

When shopping for strawberries, look for small, fragrant berries that are a rich, glossy red and have shiny green leaves. Avoid giant supermarket berries or berries with white or green shoulders and brown and limp leaves; these usually lack flavor. To clean the berries, gently brush off any sand or dirt and rinse briefly under cool running water. To hull strawberries, use a small paring knife or strawberry huller to carve out the leaves and white center core from the stem end of each berry.

1 rolled-out Basic Tart Dough round (page 111)

FOR THE PASTRY CREAM:

2 cups (16 fl oz/500 ml) whole milk

6 large egg yolks

½ cup (4 oz/125 g) sugar

¼ cup (1 oz/30 g) cornstarch (cornflour)

⅛ teaspoon salt

1 teaspoon vanilla extract (essence)

FOR THE TOPPING:

1 cup (4 oz/125 g) strawberries, hulled and cut into ½-inch (12-mm) chunks

1 cup (6 oz/185 g) red seedless grapes, halved lengthwise

1 cup (6 oz/185 g) green seedless grapes, halved lengthwise

1 cup (4 oz/125 g) fresh or thawed frozen blueberries

¼ cup (2½ oz/75 g) apricot jam

TARTE TATIN

1 rolled-out Basic Pie
Dough round (page 110)

8 large, firm, tart apples
(page 40), peeled, halved
lengthwise, and cored

1 cup (8 oz/250 g) sugar

2 tablespoons cold
unsalted butter, cut
into small pieces

Sweetened Whipped
Cream (page 111) or vanilla
ice cream for serving

Trim the dough round to 10 inches (25 cm) in diameter. Set aside
in a cool place until ready to use. Place an oven rack in the middle
of the oven and preheat to 375°F (190°C).

Thinly slice the apple halves crosswise, keeping each half together.
Pour the sugar evenly into a 10-inch (25-cm) nonstick, ovenproof
frying pan. Pack the apples, core side up, close together in the
bottom of the frying pan, using your hand to flatten and fan each
half slightly. Dot the apples with the butter and carefully place the
pie dough round over them, letting the dough hang over the sides
of the pan.

Bake until the edges of the crust are golden brown and the apples
are tender when pierced with a knife, 1–1½ hours. Remove from
the oven and let rest for 3–5 minutes. Wearing oven mitts, give the
pan a shake and place a large flat serving plate upside down
on top of the pan. Quickly invert the pan and plate together. Be
careful, as the pan and juices will still be very hot. Lift off the pan.
Using a small spatula or knife, smooth the apples. Let cool slightly.

Serve warm, accompanied with a dollop of whipped cream or a
scoop of ice cream.

MAKES ONE 10-INCH (25-CM) TART, OR 8 SERVINGS

BUTTER STYLES
Good-quality unsalted butter
is always fresher and more
flavorful than salted butter.
Do not be misled by the term
sweet cream butter; all butter
is made from sweet, not
sour, cream. Therefore, a
sweet-cream butter may be
salted. Whipped butter has
air whipped into it and should
not be used in baking recipes.
European-style butters
generally have a higher fat
content. They are perfect for
spreading on warm baked
goods or for adding to sauces
or buttercreams, but may
throw off a recipe, so use
caution when substituting in
cake and pastry recipes.

PINEAPPLE–BROWN SUGAR GALETTE

Cut the pineapple into slices ¼ inch (6 mm) thick; you should have 8–10 slices. Using a small knife or cookie cutter, remove the core from each slice to make a ring.

Place the dough round on a baking sheet lined with parchment (baking) paper. Overlap the pineapple rings in a spiral on the round, leaving a 1½-inch (4-cm) border of dough uncovered along the edge. Fold the edges of the dough up and over the pineapple, pleating the dough loosely all around the edges and leaving the galette open in the center (page 97). Sprinkle the pineapple evenly with the brown sugar, using all of it if the pineapple is tart, and dot with the butter.

Measure the circumference of the galette and cut a strip of aluminum foil about 2 inches (5 cm) longer and 3–4 inches (7.5–10 cm) wide. Fold the strip in half lengthwise, place it around the edge of the galette, and secure the ends by folding or pinching them together. (The foil helps keep the dough from unfolding.)

Refrigerate the galette until the dough is firm, 20–30 minutes. Meanwhile, place an oven rack in the lower third of the oven and preheat to 400°F (200°C).

Bake the galette until the crust is golden brown and the pineapple is tender when pierced with a fork, about 50 minutes. Transfer the baking sheet to a wire rack and let the galette cool slightly. Cut the galette into wedges and serve warm.

MAKES ONE 9-INCH (23-CM) GALETTE, OR 8 SERVINGS

1 pineapple, trimmed *(far left)*

1 rolled-out Basic Pie Dough round (page 110)

3–4 tablespoons firmly packed light brown sugar

1 tablespoon cold unsalted butter, cut into small pieces

TRIMMING PINEAPPLE
Pineapple has skin with a bumpy spiral pattern that must be removed before eating. Using a sharp knife, cut off the leaves at the top and slice off the bottom end. Holding the pineapple upright, slice off the skin just below the surface in long vertical strips, following the contour of the fruit and leaving the small brown eyes. Lay the pineapple on its side. Align the knife blade with the diagonal rows of eyes and cut shallow furrows, following a spiral pattern, to remove all of the eyes.

PIE & TART BASICS

Fresh berries encased in flaky, buttery pastry, creamy lemon custard in a pretty fluted shell, figs snugly packed in a free-form round—pies and tarts come in many shapes and flavors. And, when made with top-quality ingredients, such as fruits at their peak of ripeness, fine chocolate, or fresh cream, they suit any occasion at any time of the year, from a casual summer picnic to an elegant holiday celebration.

EQUIPMENT

The making of pies and tarts relies on similar equipment that every home baker will want to keep on hand.

Pies are usually baked in pans or dishes with sloping sides. For pies with a top and bottom crust, also known as double-crust pies, a metal pie pan, preferably aluminum, is best. Metal is an excellent heat conductor, and using a metal pan will produce a crisp, golden crust.

Glass pie dishes are also a good choice. However, because a glass dish doesn't conduct heat quite as well as a metal pan, it may take up to 10 or 15 minutes longer for the bottom crust to bake. An advantage to glass dishes is that they let you see how the bottom crust is browning.

Deep-dish glass, ceramic, or porcelain pie dishes are attractive choices for serving pies. But keep in mind that they are often deeper and wider than the standard 9-inch (23-cm) pie pans and dishes called for throughout this book. (A standard pan is about 1½ inches/4 cm deep). This means that a pie made in deep-dish glass, ceramic, or porcelain dish will require more filling.

Like glass, ceramic and porcelain also conduct heat less effectively than metal, and pies may take longer to bake in these dishes. Yet, for this reason they are an especially good choice for deep-dish fruit pies without bottom crusts, because both ceramic and porcelain will help prevent the filling from scorching.

Tarts, which almost always have only a bottom crust, are baked in tart pans with plain or fluted, vertical sides. Look for one with a removable bottom, which allows you to free a tart easily from its pan and place it on a plate for easier serving. To remove the finished tart, place the pan on a large aluminum can or canister and let the sides fall away. The pans are available in a variety of sizes. Most of the tart recipes in this book call for a 9½-inch (24-cm) round pan, but many of the recipes can also be made in a 13¾-by-4¼-inch (35-by-11-cm) rectangular pan. Small tartlet pans, measuring 2 or 4 inches (5 or 10 cm) in diameter, are also available.

A good, sturdy rolling pin is indispensable to the pie and tart baker. Not only essential for rolling out dough, a rolling pin also comes in handy for trimming the excess pastry from a tart shell. Once the dough has been fitted into the tart pan, gently roll the pin across the top of the pan to trim away the extra dough. A well-equipped baker will also want to keep pie weights on hand for blind baking crusts (page 109). For more information on rolling pins and pie weights see page 114.

GETTING STARTED

Organization and attention to detail are essential to pie and tart baking. First, carefully read through a recipe of choice from start to finish. Note chilling and baking times, and check that you have every ingredient and piece of equipment on hand. Next, gather and prepare all the ingredients.

Use only top-quality ingredients for the best results. For pastry dough, use unsalted butter, which tastes fresher than salted. Unbleached all-purpose (plain) flour is preferred because its protein content produces a particularly flaky, tender crust. Since it is not treated to chemical bleaching, it has a better flavor than standard all-purpose flour.

When making fillings, avoid using ultrapasteurized heavy (double) cream, which has a slight cooked taste. You may use bittersweet and semisweet (plain) chocolate interchangeably in the recipes in this book (the latter is slightly sweeter); purchase the best quality you can afford. Select firm, full-flavored fruits, avoiding overripe specimens that may prevent the finished pie from setting up properly.

MEASURING

Accurate measuring contributes to a successful pie or tart. Even slightly wrong proportions of flour, fat, and liquid can produce a less-than-ideal crust. For dry ingredients such as flour and sugar, use dry cup measures, graduated cups made of stainless steel or heavy-duty plastic. Spoon the dry ingredient into the measuring cup, overfilling it, and sweep the top level with the straight edge of a knife. When measuring brown sugar, press it firmly enough into the cup that it retains its shape when tapped out.

Measure wet ingredients in liquid measuring cups, which are typically made of clear glass or plastic and have measures printed vertically on the sides and a handy pouring spout. Fill the cup with the desired amount, set it on a flat surface to settle the liquid, and read it at eye level.

MIXING

Cutting butter into the flour mixture is a key step in making a good pie or tart crust. The butter must be very cold and hard and in pea-sized pieces before the liquid (usually ice water) is added. If the butter warms up and softens, the flour will absorb it, become sticky, and ultimately yield a tough crust. For the best results, start with butter taken directly from the refrigerator and work quickly. Before adding the ice water, test the butter's temperature by briefly pinching a little of the flour mixture. If the small butter chunks are cold, your fingers will be grease free; if the butter chunks are too soft, your fingers will feel slick. If the butter is too soft, refrigerate the flour-butter mixture for about 30 minutes before proceeding.

ROLLING OUT DOUGH

On a lightly floured board, flatten the dough disk with 6–8 gentle taps of the rolling pin. Lift the dough and give it a one-quarter turn. Dust the top of the dough or the rolling pin with more flour as needed.

Begin rolling from the middle of the dough round, pushing outward and stopping the pressure ¼ inch (6 mm) from the edge so that the edge does not get too thin. Lift the dough, give it a quarter turn, and repeat rolling. Use this frequent lifting and turning of the dough as a chance to gauge the thickness and to dust the work surface and dough lightly with flour. Roll the dough out about ⅛ inch (3 mm) thick. If the dough tears, dampen the edges of the tear with water, overlap them, and roll the seam together, dusting with flour.

TRANSFERRING DOUGH

Transferring a rolled-out dough round to a pan can be tricky, especially for beginners. But it is a step that gets easier with practice. The following instructions will help guide you.

TRANSFERRING DOUGH FOR PIES

Using a small, sharp knife, cut out a round 3 inches (7.5 cm) greater in diameter than your pie pan. Fold the dough round in half and transfer it to the pan, spreading your fingers underneath it for support. Gently ease the folded round into the pan, unfold it, and, being careful not to stretch the dough, pat it firmly into the bottom and up the sides. (If it stretches, it will shrink during baking.) Using kitchen scissors, trim the edge of the dough, leaving ¾ inch (2 cm) of overhang. If making a single-crust pie, fold the overhang underneath itself and pinch to create a high edge on the pan's rim. If making a double-crust pie, leave the overhang until you have filled the pie and positioned the second dough round over the top.

TRANSFERRING DOUGH FOR TARTS AND TARTLETS

Using a small, sharp knife, cut out a round 2 inches (5 cm) greater in diameter than your tart pan; if using a rectangular pan, cut out a rectangle 2 inches larger on all sides than the pan. Fold the dough in half and transfer to the pan, spreading your fingers underneath it for support. Gently ease the folded dough into the pan, unfold it, and, being careful not to stretch the dough, pat it firmly into the bottom and up the sides, letting any excess fall over the rim. Trim off the excess dough by gently running a rolling pin across the top of the pan. Press the dough into the sides to extend it slightly above the rim to help offset shrinkage during baking.

If making tartlets, roll out a 12-inch (30-cm) round. To make

4-inch (10-cm) tartlets, use a 6-inch (15-cm) cardboard circle or other template and a small, sharp knife to cut out 3 or 4 rounds. Press the dough scraps together and reroll to cut out additional rounds. To make 2-inch (5-cm) tartlets, use a 2½- or 3-inch (6- or 7.5-cm) cookie cutter or other template to cut out the rounds.

FLUTING AND CRIMPING

Fluting the rim of a single-crust pie adds a pretty edge, while fluting or crimping a double-crust pie seals the bottom and top crusts together, which prevents the filling from oozing out as the pie bakes, and creates a decorative finish.

FLUTING SINGLE-CRUST PIES

To flute the edge of the dough, pinch the folded edge between the index finger of your nondominant hand and the index finger and thumb of your dominant hand every 2–3 inches (5–7.5 cm) to form a scalloped edge. Or, with a thumb on top of the rim and a forefinger underneath, pinch together the dough edges, pressing the thumb down into the dough.

CRIMPING AND FLUTING DOUBLE-CRUST PIES

Both crimping and fluting begin with tucking about 1 inch (2.5 cm) of the

top dough round under the bottom dough round. Crimping is then usually done with a fork or pastry crimper (see page 10), whereas fluting the edge of a double-crust pie is done in the same manner as for a single-crust pie.

Once the dough has been formed in its pan, refrigerate or freeze it before baking until well chilled, about 30 minutes. This step prevents shrinkage.

DECORATING

Decorating pies and tarts can as simple as adding a dollop of whipped cream or a scoop of vanilla ice cream. For a more elegant look, try piping the cream (page 111).

Pastry cutouts also add a pretty touch. Reserve any scraps from the crusts, roll them out, and cut out decorative shapes with a small knife or cookie cutters. For double-crust pies, moisten the undersides of the cutouts with cold water and arrange them attractively on the top crust. For single-crust pies, sprinkle the cutouts with sugar and bake in a 350°F (180°C) oven until golden brown, 10–12 minutes. Let cool and place on the surface of the cooled baked pie.

For double-crust pies, instead of cutting steam vents, use small cookie cutters to make a pattern of pretty holes in the top crust before you place it over the filling.

MAKING A LATTICE TOP

Weaving pastry strips together into a lattice on top of a filled pie is a pretty way to create a decorative, golden crust. Shown opposite are the steps for making a lattice top.

Follow the Basic Pie Dough recipe for rolling out a rectangle for a lattice top (page 110). Leave the trimmed overhang of the bottom crust until the lattice is finished.

1 Starting at the short end and using a pastry wheel or small, sharp knife, cut the rectangle into 16 strips, each about ¾ inch (2 cm) wide. Lay about 8 of the strips across the filled pie shell horizontally. Think of the top strip as number 1 and the bottom strip as number 8.

2 Fold strips 2, 4, 6, and 8 back onto themselves to your left. Lay a vertical strip down the center at a slight angle. Unfold the strips.

3 Fold strips 1, 3, 5, and 7 onto themselves to your left. Lay a vertical strip to the right of the center strip. Unfold the strips.

4 Fold strips 1, 3, 5, and 7 onto themselves to your right. Lay a vertical strip to the left of the center strip. Unfold the strips.

Add the remaining strips to both sides of the pie in the same manner. Trim the edges of the strips even with the rim of the pan. Fold the overhang from the bottom dough round up and over the edges of the lattice and crimp to seal (page 107). Alternatively, fold the lattice and overhang underneath themselves to form a rim and press gently to seal.

PARTIALLY AND FULLY BAKING CRUSTS

Some pie and tart recipes call for fully or partially baking the crust before filling it. This is especially true for recipes with fillings that need limited or no further cooking or with juicy fillings that could make an uncooked bottom crust soggy. This step is also known as blind baking or prebaking.

To partially or fully bake pie, tart, or tartlet shells, place an oven rack in the lower third of the oven and preheat to 375°F (190°C). Remove the pastry shell or shells from the refrigerator or freezer. Line with a sheet of aluminum foil or parchment (baking) paper large enough to over-hang the sides, patting it into the bottom and up and over the sides of the dough. Cover the bottom of the shell with a generous layer of pie weights (page 114) or raw short-grain rice. The weights keep the crust from bubbling and help prevent shrinkage.

For a partially baked pie or tart shell, bake for 20 minutes, then lift an edge of the foil to check the dough. If it looks wet, continue to bake, checking it every 5 minutes, until the dough is pale gold. The total baking time will be 25–30 minutes.

For a fully baked pie or tart shell, remove the weights and foil. Return the shell to the oven and continue to bake until golden, 7–10 minutes longer, for a total baking time of 30–40 minutes.

For fully baked tartlet shells, bake the weighted shells as directed for the pie or tart shell until they are a pale gold, but reduce the initial baking time to 15 minutes. Remove the weights and foil and continue to bake until golden, 5 minutes longer, for a total baking time of 20–25 minutes.

If bubbles form in the crust during baking, press them down with a fork. Do not prick them, or you may create holes in the bottom crust through which filling can seep.

BAKING

Accurate heat levels are important when baking. It is a good idea to use an oven thermometer to check your oven's accuracy. If the oven is off by 25° or 50°F (5° or 10°C), adjust the temperature accordingly. If the edges of a crust are browning too fast, shield them during the final minutes of baking with a circle of aluminum foil strips arranged shiny side out.

SERVING

Some pies and tarts must be allowed to cool completely or be refrigerated for the filling to set properly. Follow the serving instructions in each recipe for the best results.

BASIC RECIPES

Following are the basic recipes called for throughout this book. The pie dough is tender and flaky and will yield a crust with a buttery, slightly sweet flavor, whereas the tart dough is sturdier and has a more cookielike quality.

COOKIE CRUMB CRUST

1¼ cups (4 oz/125 g) cookie crumbs such as graham crackers, chocolate wafers, or gingersnaps

5 tablespoons (2½ oz/75 g) unsalted butter, melted

3 tablespoons sugar

Place an oven rack in the middle of the oven and preheat to 350°F (180°C).

In a bowl, combine the cookie crumbs, melted butter, and sugar and stir until the crumbs are well moistened. Pat the mixture firmly and evenly into the bottom and all the way up the sides of a 9-inch (23-cm) pie pan or dish.

Bake until the crust is firm, about 5 minutes. For a firmer, crunchier crust, bake for an additional 5 minutes. Makes one 9-inch (23-cm) crust.

BASIC PIE DOUGH

1¼ cups (6½ oz/200 g) unbleached all-purpose (plain) flour

1 tablespoon sugar

¼ teaspoon salt

½ cup (4 oz/125 g) cold unsalted butter, cut into ¼-inch (6-mm) cubes

3 tablespoons very cold water

To make the dough by hand, in a large bowl, stir together the flour, sugar, and salt. Using a pastry cutter or two knives, cut the butter into the flour mixture until the texture resembles coarse cornmeal, with butter pieces no larger than small peas. Add the water and mix with a fork just until the dough pulls together.

To make the dough in a stand mixer fitted with the paddle attachment, stir together the flour, sugar, and salt in the mixer bowl. Add the butter and toss with a fork to coat with the flour mixture. Mix on medium-low speed until the texture resembles coarse cornmeal, with the butter pieces no larger than small peas. Add the water and mix on low speed just until the dough pulls together.

Transfer the dough to a work surface, pat into a ball, and flatten into a disk. (Although many dough recipes call for chilling the dough at this point, this dough should be rolled out immediately for the best results.) Lightly flour the work surface, then flatten the disk with 6–8 gentle taps of the rolling pin. Lift the dough and give it a quarter turn. Lightly dust the top of the dough or the rolling pin with flour as needed, then roll out as described on page 106 into a round at least 12 inches (30 cm) in diameter and about ⅛ inch (3 mm) thick. Makes enough dough for one 9-inch (23-cm) single-crust pie or one 10-inch (25-cm) galette.

To make a double-crust pie: Double the recipe, cut the dough in half, and pat each half into a round, flat disk. Roll out one disk into a 12-inch (30-cm) round as directed and line the pan or dish. Press any scraps trimmed from the first round into the bottom of the second disk. Roll out the second dough disk into a round at least 12 inches (30 cm) in diameter and about ⅛ inch (3 mm) thick and refrigerate until ready to use.

To make a lattice top: Double the recipe, cut the dough in half, and pat one half into a round, flat disk. Roll out the disk into a 12-inch (30-cm) round as directed and line the pan or dish. Trim the edge of the dough, leaving a ½-inch (12-mm) overhang. Press any scraps trimmed from the first round into the bottom of the remaining dough half. Pat the dough into a rectangle and roll out into a rectangular shape about ⅛ inch (3 mm) thick. Trim to cut out a 14-by-11-inch (35-by-28-cm) rectangle and refrigerate until ready to use.

Nut Dough Variation: Add 2 tablespoons ground toasted pecans, walnuts, almonds, or hazelnuts (filberts) to the flour mixture and proceed as directed.

Make-Ahead Tip: Pie dough may be made ahead and frozen for up to 2 months. To freeze, place the dough round on a 12-inch (30-cm) cardboard circle and wrap it well with plastic wrap. Alternatively, use the round to line a pie pan or dish, flute the edge, and wrap well.

BASIC TART DOUGH

1 large egg yolk

2 tablespoons very cold water

1 teaspoon vanilla extract (essence)

1¼ cups (6½ oz/200 g) unbleached all-purpose (plain) flour

⅓ cup (3 oz/90 g) sugar

¼ teaspoon salt

½ cup (4 oz/125 g) cold unsalted butter, cut into ¼-inch (6-mm) cubes

In a small bowl, stir together the egg yolk, water, and vanilla. Set aside.

To make the dough by hand, in a large bowl, stir together the flour, sugar, and salt. Using a pastry cutter or two knives, cut the butter into the flour mixture until the texture resembles coarse cornmeal, with butter pieces no larger than small peas. Add the egg mixture and mix with a fork just until the dough pulls together.

To make the dough in a stand mixer fitted with the paddle attachment, stir together the flour, sugar, and salt in the mixer bowl. Add the butter and mix on medium-low speed until the texture resembles coarse cornmeal, with butter pieces no larger than small peas. Add the egg mixture and mix just until the dough pulls together.

Transfer the dough to a work surface, pat into a ball, and flatten into a disk. The dough may be used immediately or wrapped in plastic wrap and refrigerated until well chilled, about 30 minutes.

To roll out the dough, on a lightly floured board, flatten the disk with 6–8 gentle taps of the rolling pin. Lift the dough and give it a quarter turn. Lightly dust the top of the dough or the rolling pin with flour as needed, then roll out as described on page 106 until the dough is about ⅛ inch (3 mm) thick. Use a small, sharp knife to cut out a round or rounds 2 inches greater in diameter than your tart or larger tartlet pans. Use a small, sharp knife or a cookie cutter to cut out rounds ½–1 inch (12 mm–2.5 cm) greater in diameter than your miniature tartlet pans. If using a rectangular tart pan, cut out a rectangle 2 inches (5 cm) larger on all sides than the pan. Makes enough dough for one 9½-inch (24-cm) tart, six 4-inch (10-cm) tartlets, twelve 2-inch (5-cm) miniature tartlets, or one 13¾-by-4¼-inch (35-by-11-cm) rectangular tart.

Nut Dough Variation: Add 2 tablespoons ground toasted pecans, walnuts, almonds, or hazelnuts (filberts) to the flour mixture and proceed as directed.

Make-Ahead Tip: Tart dough may be made ahead and frozen for up to 1 month. To freeze, place the dough round on a 12-inch (30-cm) cardboard circle and wrap it well with plastic wrap. Alternatively, use the round to line a tart pan and wrap well.

SWEETENED WHIPPED CREAM

1 cup (8 fl oz/250 ml) heavy (double) cream

1 tablespoon sugar

1 teaspoon vanilla extract (essence)

In a deep bowl, combine the cream, sugar, and vanilla. Using an electric mixer set on medium-high speed, beat until soft, billowy peaks form, about 2 minutes. Cover the bowl and refrigerate until serving or for up to 2 hours. Makes about 2 cups (16 fl oz/ 500 ml).

To pipe the whipped cream onto the surface of a pie or tart, continue to beat the cream until firm peaks form, about 1 minute longer. Fit a 12-inch (30-cm) pastry bag with a ¼-inch (6-mm) plain or star tip. Just above the tip, give the bag a few twists and push it into the tip to close off the opening. Fold the top of the bag over to form a 3-inch (7.5-cm) cuff. Slide one hand under the cuff to support the bag, then scoop the whipped cream into the bag, filling it half full. Unfold the cuff and twist the top until the bag is taut and the tip is full. Hold the tip at a 45-degree angle close to the pie or tart and squeeze to make rosettes or other patterns.

GLOSSARY

BLUEBERRIES Two primary types of blueberries are harvested, high bush and low bush. High-bush berries, which are the common cultivated blueberries, are large and have smooth, dark blue skin, a powdery white bloom, and pale flesh. The low-bush, or wild, blueberry, which is found primarily in Maine and Canada, is a small, deep blue fruit with sweet, blue flesh. It is excellent to use in pies. So-called wild blueberries have been domesticated, but the supply is limited.

CHIFFON A type of filling for pies, chiffon is revered for its light and fluffy qualities. The Citrus Chiffon Pie in this book (page 63) is made with whipped cream that has been stabilized by gelatin.

CONDENSED MILK See page 68.

CORNSTARCH Also called cornflour, cornstarch is a highly refined, silky powder ground from the endosperm of corn—the white heart of the kernel. It is used as a neutral-flavored thickening agent in fruit fillings, puddings, and glazes. Fillings and glazes thickened with cornstarch have a glossy sheen, unlike those thickened with flour, which are opaque. Recipes that call for cornstarch require cooking to eliminate any starchy taste.

CORN SYRUP This syrup, made from cornstarch, is used to sweeten some pie and tart fillings. Available in dark and light versions, it will not crystallize when heated. Dark corn syrup has more flavor than light syrup; it's generally best to use what a recipe directs.

CRANBERRIES Native to North America, cranberries grow on thick vines in bogs layered with sand, peat, and clay. Harvested throughout the autumn months, they are cultivated in New Jersey, Massachusetts, Wisconsin, Oregon, Washington, British Columbia, and Quebec. When cranberries are added to the sweet custard or other sweet filling of a pie or tart, their natural tartness provides a welcome counterpoint. Fresh cranberries, which range from deep scarlet to light red, should be plump, firm, and dry. Both fresh and frozen whole berries are usually packaged in plastic bags rather than sold loose.

CURD A thick, custardlike pie or tart filling made from eggs, curd is often flavored with the juice and zest of citrus fruit (see page 78).

CUSTARD A thick, rich, sweet mixture that has long been used as a filling for pies, custard is made by gently cooking together eggs, sugar, and milk or cream, as well as other ingredients.

DOUBLE BOILER See page 25.

EGGS, RAW Eggs are sometimes used raw or partially cooked in meringue and other preparations. These eggs run a risk of being infected with salmonella or other bacteria, which can lead to food poisoning. This risk is of most concern to small children, older people, pregnant women, and anyone with a compromised immune system. If you have health and safety concerns, do not consume raw eggs. Once pasteurized, raw eggs can be eaten with no ill effects.

To make eggs safe to consume, break them into a heatproof bowl and whisk to blend. Set the bowl over, but not touching, simmering water in a pan; the bowl should sit 1 inch (2.5 cm) above the water. Cook, stirring constantly, until the mixture reaches 140°F (60°C). Maintain the temperature of the mixture between 140°F and 150°F (60° and 66°C) for 5 minutes. (If the mixture climbs above 150°F, remove from the heat.) Place the bowl over an ice bath, and stir the eggs with a spatula until cool. These eggs can be used when making the fillings for Citrus Chiffon Pie (page 63) or Raspberry Cream Pie (page 71).

EGGS, SEPARATING Eggs are easier to separate when cold. Carefully crack each egg and, holding it over a bowl, pass the yolk back and forth between the shell halves and let the whites fall into the bowl. Drop the yolk into a separate bowl, and transfer the whites to a third bowl.

Separate each additional egg over an empty bowl, for if any speck of yolk gets into the whites, the whites will not whip up properly. If a yolk breaks, start fresh with another egg.

GELATIN See page 63.

KITCHEN SCISSORS Every baker should have at least one pair of stainless-steel scissors in their kitchen to use for neatly trimming dough around the edges of a pie pan. They are also handy for cutting parchment paper.

NONALUMINUM See page 78.

NUTS, GRINDING To grind nuts, use a hand-cranked nut mill or process in a food processor using short pulses. If using a food processor, beware of over-processing the nuts into a smooth paste, which releases their oils and diminishes their flavor. For best results, combine the nuts with a little of the flour or sugar called for in the recipe and process for no longer than 5 to 10 seconds at a time.

NUTS, TOASTING Toasting nuts will intensify their flavor and give them a crisp texture and attractive golden color. To toast nuts, spread them in a single layer on a baking sheet and bake them in a 325°F (165°C) oven, stirring occasionally to prevent overbrowning, until the nuts are golden and fragrant. Depending on the type of nut and size of the pieces, this may take 10 to 20 minutes. Remove the nuts from the pan as soon as they start to brown, pouring them onto a plate and letting them cool. They will continue to cook slightly after removal from the pan. Or, toast nuts in a small, dry frying pan over medium heat. Shake the pan often, and remove the nuts when they start to brown.

PARCHMENT PAPER See page 90.

PASTRY CREAM A thick, creamy custard, pastry cream is often used as a base for fresh fruit tarts.

PASTRY CRIMPER Resembling large tweezers and sold in different patterns, pastry crimpers are used to seal together the top and bottom crusts of pies and other filled pastries. The most common type is made of stainless steel and has serrated edges.

PASTRY CUTTER Also called a pastry blender, this tool is used to cut butter into flour for a flaky pie crust. It has a wooden or plastic handle anchoring a row of metal blades or wires forming a U shape. The blades or wires act as cutters, reducing pieces of butter or other fat mixed with flour to the size of small peas or the consistency of coarse meal. A pastry cutter with blades is preferred for making the dough recipes in this book.

PASTRY WHEEL This tool is used to cut out or trim rolled-out pastry dough, especially strips for lattice tops. Pastry wheels are circular and may have straight or fluted edges attached to a handle that lets you roll them across the dough. They are sometimes referred to as pastry jaggers for their jagged edges.

PIE WEIGHTS Also known as pastry weights, these small aluminum or ceramic pellets are used, along with parchment (baking) paper or aluminum foil, to weight down pastry dough when it is partially or fully baked (page 109). Raw short-grain rice will work in their place, but do not use dried beans, which some bakers recommend. In the heat of the oven, they give off a bad odor and their skins begin to flake. If blind baking 2-inch (5-cm) tartlets, paper muffin-cup liners and coins are a quick and easy substitute for parchment paper and pie weights.

RICOTTA This soft cheese can be found in plastic containers in the dairy section of most well-stocked markets. It is made by heating the whey left over from making sheep's, goat's, or cow's milk cheeses. Most Italian ricotta is made from sheep's milk. When sweetened and mixed with other ingredients, it can be used as a base for a rustic galette (page 93).

ROLLING PIN Chief among the most essential tools for pie and tart bakers, rolling pins come in various styles. A heavy, smooth hardwood or marble pin at least 15 inches (38 cm) long is best. Some bakers prefer a French-style pin without handles, either a straight dowel or a dowel with tapered ends, while others prefer pins with handles.

If you choose the latter, look for one with handles that move on ball bearings for the smoothest roll.

RUBBER SPATULA This handy kitchen tool is used for stirring, folding, and scraping. The best ones have blades made of silicone rubber, which won't melt or stick when used in a hot pan. Avoid plastic ones. Have a few different sizes on hand for different tasks.

SPICES
Essential oils are the source of flavor in spices, but they will evaporate over time, so replace your spices periodically. If stored in tightly closed containers in a cool, dark place, ground spices will keep for about 6 months and whole spices for about 1 year. Purchase spices in small amounts from stores with high turnover, and label them with the date of purchase. For the most pronounced flavor, use whole spices and grind them fresh.

Allspice: The berry of an evergreen tree, allspice tastes like a combination of cinnamon, nutmeg, and cloves, hence its name.

Cardamom: This intense spice is the dried fruit of a plant in the ginger family. Cardamom is highly aromatic and has an exotic flavor. Its small, round seeds, which come enclosed in a husklike pod, may be purchased whole or already ground.

Cinnamon: The dark bark of a tree, the most commonly found variety is cassia cinnamon, which is a dark red-brown and has a strong, sweet taste. Cinnamon is available in stick form or already ground. If you grind your own cinnamon, first break or crush the stick into pieces.

Cloves: Shaped like a small nail with a round head, the almost-black clove is the dried bud of a tropical evergreen tree. It has a strong, sweet flavor with a peppery quality and is available whole or ground.

Nutmeg: The oval brown seed of a soft fruit, a nutmeg has a hard shell that is in turn covered by the membrane that becomes mace. A beloved spice, it has a warm, sweet flavor. Whole nutmeg keeps its flavor much longer than ground, and can be freshly grated as needed with a special nutmeg or other fine grater.

TAPIOCA A starchy substance derived from the root of the cassava plant, tapioca can be used to thicken fruit fillings for pies. Tapioca comes in three basic forms, pearl (small dried balls of tapioca starch), granulated (coarsely broken-up pearl tapioca), or quick-cooking, also called instant (very finely granulated pearl tapioca).

VANILLA Lending perfume, depth, and nuance to a wide variety of baked goods, vanilla may be used either in its whole-bean form or as vanilla extract.

A vanilla bean is the cured pod of a type of climbing orchid. There are three primary types of vanilla beans: Bourbon-Madagascar, Tahitian, and Mexican.

Bourbon-Madagascar beans, the most common, make up about three-fourths of the world's supply of vanilla. They have a stronger flavor than the more floral Tahitian beans. Mexican beans carry the boldest flavor of the three. Some Mexican beans are known to contain coumarin, however, a substance that can be toxic, so purchase them only from a reputable source. Most recipes call for a whole or half vanilla bean split lengthwise. Splitting the pod allows the tiny seeds to escape and their flavor to permeate a dish.

Vanilla extract, also known as vanilla essence, is made by chopping the beans and soaking them in a mixture of alcohol and water, then aging the solution. Avoid imitation vanilla, which is made of artificial flavorings and has an inferior taste. Vanilla extract is most often made from Bourbon-Madagascar beans, and the best-quality vanilla extracts should state this on their label.

WHISKS With a head of looped thin metal wires, a whisk is essential for blending custard fillings and beating egg whites. Use a smaller, less open sauce whisk with a long, tapered shape for custards, and a balloon whisk for whipping egg whites. Balloon whisks have more wires than sauce whisks. Their wires are also thinner and taper into a rounded ball shape.

INDEX

SIMON & SCHUSTER SOURCE
A Division of Simon & Schuster, Inc.
1230 Avenue of the Americas
New York, NY 10020

WILLIAMS-SONOMA
Founder and Vice-Chairman: Chuck Williams

WELDON OWEN INC.
Chief Executive Officer: John Owen
President: Terry Newell
Chief Operating Officer: Larry Partington
Vice President, International Sales: Stuart Laurence
Creative Director: Gaye Allen
Series Editor: Sarah Putman Clegg
Editor: Heather Belt
Designer: Teri Gardiner
Production Manager: Chris Hemesath
Production Assistant: Libby Temple

Weldon Owen wishes to thank
the following people for their generous
assistance and support in producing
this book: Copy Editor Carolyn Krebs;
Consulting Editors Sharon Silva and Judith Dunham;
Food Stylists Kim Konecny and Erin Quon;
Photographer's Assistant Faiza Ali; Proofreaders
Desne Ahlers and Arin Hailey; Indexer Ken DellaPenta;
and Production Designer Joan Olson.

Set in Trajan, Utopia, and Vectora.

Williams-Sonoma Collection *Pie & Tart* was
conceived and produced by Weldon Owen Inc.,
814 Montgomery Street, San Francisco,
California 94133, in collaboration with
Williams-Sonoma, 3250 Van Ness Avenue,
San Francisco, California 94109.

A Weldon Owen Production
Copyright © 2003 by Weldon Owen Inc. and
Williams-Sonoma Inc.

For information about special discounts for bulk
purchases, please contact Simon & Schuster
Special Sales: 1-800-456-6798 or
business@simonandschuster.com

Color separations by Bright Arts Graphics
Singapore (Pte.) Ltd.
Printed and bound in Singapore by Tien Wah
Press (Pte.) Ltd.

First printed in 2003.

10 9 8 7 6 5

Library of Congress Cataloging-in-Publication
Data is available.

ISBN 0-7432-4316-1

A NOTE ON WEIGHTS AND MEASURES

All recipes include customary U.S. and metric measurements. Metric conversions are based on
a standard developed for these books and have been rounded off. Actual weights may vary.